The Quakers Meeting

LET YOUR LIFE SPEAK

"In returning and rest shall ye be saved, in quietness and in confidence shall be your strength."

Isaiah 30:15

"'The divine principle in man is given, not for the gratification of our curiosity, but for the government of our lives.' Were this kept in view, the tone of the preaching on this day of the week would be changed. Abstract theories, as well as the attempted descriptions of a future world, would give place to the enforcing of the great practical duties of life."

Lucretia Mott, *Lucretia Mott Speaks.*

"I have never been accustomed to look at the Bible as a plenary inspiration, but I love these Scriptures, and love to find their testimonies to the truth in every age of which they treat. I love to find also among other ages and other people the same testimonies to the truth and to righteousness. They all tend to strengthen, to give force, to prove that they claimed and observed these teachings in every condition and operation of the mind as able to act, to convert, to adjust to the level of all these attributes of the Deity. For these instinctive principles of our higher nature are all by which we can claim to touch the Almighty."

Lucretia Mott, *Lucretia Mott Speaks.*

Thirty-Three Ways Seven Faiths Agree with the Quakers

by Thomas Wolfe R.H.
and Companions

Published by
Be Friendly Ministries

Hardcover Edition

Copyright © 2024 by Thomas Wolfe.

All quotes not in Public Domain used with permission.

All rights reserved. No part of this book may be reproduced in any form or by any means, electronic or mechanical, including photocopying, recording, or by any information storage and retrieval system, without permission in writing from the publisher.

Cover design by Karl Moeller.

ISBN: 978-1-73-652269-1

Garamond font.

First edition 2024.

BeFriendlyMinistries@gmail.com

DEDICATION

This work is dedicated to three friends:

Margaret Fell (1614-1702)
Lucretia Mott (1793-1880)
John Greenleaf Whittier (1807-1892)

"For all the souls who sought your way Oh Lord,
In silent waiting listening for thy word.
They feared no man, no priest or magistrate,
To learn from thee that Love will conquer hate."

"Oh, may we too, thus bravely seek your plan,
And valiantly speed the work which they began.
To speak to that of God in every man."
Alleluia!

Valiant For the Truth Hymn 255
"Worship in Song" A Friends Hymnal 1996 (FGC)

CONTENTS

Foreword — Patrick Nugent
Quaker Bible Study Foreword — Francis Wayne
Introduction — Thomas Wolfe
Preface — Thomas Wolfe

SECTION ONE: PEACE
Principle:
1. Peace of Mind
2. Real Surrender is Resignation to the Will of God
3. Love is Patience and Contentment
4. Love is Doing No Harm
5. Accept Happiness and Suffering with Equal Poise
6. Loving without Wanting Anything in Return

SECTION TWO: EQUALITY
Principle:
1. Self-Sacrifice
2. Love is Taking Responsibility
3. Love is Gratitude
4. Help and Serve Others
5. Humility
6. Selfless Service

SECTION THREE: SIMPLICITY
Principle:
1. Renunciation of all Selfish Thoughts and Desires
2. Real Control is Discipline of the Senses
3. Attend to Your Duties but Do Not Be Attached to Results
4. Accept What Comes to You without Resentment
5. Interest in Sensual Indulgence Naturally Falls Away
6. Renunciation
7. Obedience to What You Know to be True

CONTENTS

SECTION FOUR: TRUTH
Principle:
1. Our Real Existence is Oneness
2. Love is Living by Spiritual Principles
3. Remember God with Your Dying Breath
4. Longing for Truth and Union
5. Desperation/Passion
6. Faith
7. Surrender Wholeheartedly and without Fear

SECTION FIVE: ORDER
Principle:
1. Love is the Longing to Know More and Improve Ourselves
2. Knowledge is Equality and Nonjudgement
3. Love is Empathy
4. Love is Giving to Others
5. Love is Compassion
6. Do Not Shirk Your Responsibilities
7. Fidelity

Acknowledgments
Photo Credits

That there is Universal Light every age does testify. There is not a nation in the world, nor an age throughout all time, that is destitute of the discovery of Inner Light.

William Penn, 1668

FOREWORD

Patrick J. Nugent, Quaker Minister (Friends United Meeting)

What makes us interesting and worthwhile? The things about us that are the same as others, or the things that are different?

    I have struggled with this question my entire adult life, both in the field of religious studies and in my personal life. As an undergraduate, I became fascinated by Zen Buddhism, under the guidance of a world-renowned Catholic theologian, Paul Knitter, at Xavier University. What entranced me was all the similarities between Zen meditation and the practice of Christian contemplative prayer or "centering prayer" that I was exposed to by Jesuit mentors in high school, and practiced regularly. Almost fifteen years later, I was a professor at Earlham College, a Quaker institution in Indiana, and had become a Quaker myself. I chose Quakerism because of its pacifist commitments and the fact that it stripped away everything about Christian ritual except that contemplative, centering practice, and preaching—speaking the word of God, not out of academic preparation, but under the immediate influence of the Holy Spirit. Zen had little interest in any words or ideas that might come from meditation, but the similarities between Quaker silent worship and Zen sitting meditation remained deeply attractive to me.

    Then I had the shock of my life. Earlham sent our family to Morioka, Japan, for a semester to lead a foreign study program with a group of Earlham students. Along the way, I was to develop a course in Japanese religion that I could teach the students and then insert into my regular teaching rotation "back home in Indiana," as the song goes. As I studied Zen Buddhism, along with other schools of Japanese Buddhism and other religious communities and practices, I learned that most of Zen practice in the real world of Japanese temples has little to do with meditation and the Zen spiritual tradition. At the time, at the turn of the millennium, only ten percent of Japanese Zen temples even

FOREWORD

had a Zen-do, a meditation room. Zen, like all forms of Japanese Buddhism, is principally a system for what the fictional German theologian Franz Bibfeldt, an enduring character in the life of the Divinity School at the University of Chicago, called in a book he never wrote, "the pastoral care of the dead." Buddhist practice in Japan serves the purpose of ushering the spirits of the dead along their journey, from the funeral through a series of anniversaries over a span of years, enabling families to cultivate their memories of the dead while gradually letting them go. It's beautiful, fascinating, unlike anything I'd ever experienced in my own life, and utterly alien. I came to realize that the Zen Buddhism that is known and loved the world over is actually mostly the creation of Western practitioners of meditation in dialogue with a few Zen scholars with a heavy dose of influence from the brilliant and holy Vietnamese teacher, Thich Nhat Hanh. It is completely divorced, however, from the daily, monthly, annual round of ritual and ceremony in most Zen temples and Japan. Rubbing shoulders with these experiences was rich, delicious, inspiring, and compelling, but had nothing to do with anything in my field of spiritual interest or my Christian faith. I continue, decades later, to meditate daily and apply what I've learned from Zen, from the mindfulness tradition, and from the Western monastic tradition.

As a Quaker and a disciple of Jesus Christ who was becoming a scholar, I had a choice between a path in religious studies that explored topics directly related to my faith, and a path that explored other things. I chose the latter. I though my field of specialty would be medieval mysticism, something dear to my heart as a person who practiced and valued meditation and the direct experience of God, but I found myself instead trying to understand the religious practices of ordinary people. This was a difficult task, because ordinary people in medieval Europe didn't write anything. They only appear in the literature when literate, educated clergy wrote about them. But I found texts in which they appeared, albeit through a densely interpreted filter, and saw them engaging in religious practices that bore no relation at

FOREWORD

all to my understanding of Christianity as I practiced it. But this material—so completely different from what I cared about—was as delicious and rich and compelling as Japanese practices of caring for the dead. I approached the material as a historian using anthropological methods, learning about things that were very foreign to my own practice of Christianity and my interest in the broad arc of the Christian theological tradition. I loved it.

Along the way, I became interested in Islam. As with both Zen Buddhism and medieval Christianity, I began the journey by being fascinated by the similarities. I saw myself and my faith reflected in certain streams of Islam, particularly aspects of Sufism and of the medieval Islamic philosophical tradition. But the more I learned, the more interested I became in the aspects of Islam that were different from what I knew and valued as a Christian and a Quaker. I was inspired by the great Western scholar of Islam, Marshall Hodgson, who was also a Quaker and in fact a member of the same Friends Meeting in Chicago as I was, although two decades before. Hodgson's historical work spurred my interests in Islamic splinter groups, heresies, and fragmentation—the same themes I was working on in medieval Christianity and Japanese Buddhism.

In my journey as a Quaker, I came to learn that half of the world's Quakers live in Kenya, and that they are dramatically different from North American Quakers, especially the liberal Friends who maintain a version of the old practice of "silent worship" or "waiting on the Lord." My wife and I were invited in 2002 to move to Kenya where I would be Principal (CEO) of Friends Theological College, an institution founded in the late 1940s to train Kenyan Quaker pastors. All Kenyan Friends are theologically evangelical (as are about half of North American Friends). Most are also mildly or extravagantly Pentecostal. I found this very strange indeed. They violated almost everything I knew about what it meant to be Quaker, although I was grateful for their unyielding devotion to Christ as Savior and Lord, a feature of all Quakers until the late nineteenth century. To make matters worse, Kenya Friends at the time were plagued by the rampant and ubiquitous corruption and graft that afflicts many postcolonial nations. I served in Kenya for five years, and I had to work constantly and tirelessly to find threads of commonality and motivations for sympathy and empathy. It was very difficult.

In the end, I learned enormously from all the ways Kenyan Friends are different, and I came to understand with some sympathy the Pentecostal worldview, partly with the help of some nonreligious scholars of Pentecostalism, and partly by listening openly to things I was not open to, expressed nonetheless by people about whom I cared deeply. At several points, however, I was in danger of giving up, because it was too hard to find the commonalities and too easy to be angered by the differences.

It is common to hear people—usually Westerners who are Christian or post-Christian—say that despite all the differences between religions, we ultimately believe the same things deep down. When we say that, we value the ways in which other people are like us. We do this in daily relationships, too. Psychologists call this "mirroring." We fall in love or develop friendships because we see something of ourselves in those to whom we are attracted. After a while, however, we discover things that are different. Sometimes this becomes the nucleus of conflict and relationships can fall apart. Sometimes it becomes a stimulus to growing to greater depths.

What makes people other than ourselves interesting and valuable—the ways in which they are like us, or the ways in which they are different?

If your only value to me resides in how you resemble me, then you are only a mirror and I am Narcissus. I like having things in common with other people—don't get me wrong—but I find that things only get interesting when I begin to understand what makes them unique—in other words, different from me and perhaps from everyone else I know. Scholarly approaches to religion take a similar, although much more nuanced and sophisticated, approach. If all we look for in other religions is the way we agree, then we are making ourselves the measure of the value of others. As a scholar of religion—even if one has no religion oneself, as is true of many academic specialists in religion—putting the uniqueness and distinctiveness of the object of one's study at the center of the exploration is an act of basic respect. It says that the important thing is, as much as possible, to understand what one is studying on its own terms, not according to how it resembles what one already knows, cares about, and agrees with.

For religious people involved in interreligious dialogue, especially Westerners, this is a critical but often-neglected principle. If I value in other religions only the things that agree with my own, then I am making myself the measuring stick for the value of other people. That is cultural narcissism.

On the other hand, if I all I know or notice in other religions are the things that are different, the things with which I disagree and the things I find distasteful, and if I lack a sense of curiosity and appreciation, then I've committed the opposite offense: I fail to recognize our common humanity, I lack sympathy or empathy, and I find it easy to categories those who are different as enemies or oddities.

So I think we have to move back and forth between understanding and appreciating the things that make us similar and the things that make us different—both in our study of other religions and our relations with them, and in our personal relationships. The other dimension of my personal fascination with what makes other religions different and unique is a stance of appreciation and curiosity that precedes my exploration of what is unfamiliar and alien. Without that stance of appreciation, I risk becoming an isolationist or a bigot.

As it happens, life takes us on strange journeys, and the needs of my family meant leaving the academic world. I am now an executive in the world of nonprofit performing arts. I run an organization that combines an opera company, a ballet company, and a symphony orchestra into one organization. And guess what? I've been forced once again beyond the boundaries of

FOREWORD

what I know and love best (classical orchestra music and aspects of ballet) to explore and understand with empathy the things that I find foreign or alien (opera as a genre, and the troubled relationship between the art of ballet and the care of the human body and soul).

* * * *

I first met Tom Wolfe at gatherings of the Illinois Yearly Meeting of the Religious Society of Friends (a yearly meeting being something akin to a diocese or a conference or a synod in other Protestant communities) in the late 1980s. I found him open, curious, learned, empathetic, yet committed to his own understanding of Quakerism and Christian faith—parts of which were very akin to mine, andparts substantially different. (I can't escape this theme.) We then crossed paths again in 2015 when my wife and I began a four-year period of living near Annapolis Maryland and attending the Annapolis Friends Meeting, of which Tom is a pillar and spiritual leader. At that time I learned in much greater depth about deep commonalities in our approaches to Quakerism and Christianity, although I also came to learn that he had a deep interest in other religious traditions in ways that were very new to me, but intriguing nonetheless. Tom is squarely and deeply committed to illustrating how different religious traditions or teachers agree with one another. He has a series of books that have done this brilliantly and with an idiosyncrasy that I find absolutely delicious, rich, and compelling. Nobody does it the way that Tom does, and I love that. So when he asked me to write the Foreword to a new book on thirty-three ways in which seven religious traditions agreed with Quakerism, I was delighted. I love the Quaker tradition, and I love how Tom lets it speak for itself in its own words.

The Quaker tradition is not simple or uniform. I am deeply disappointed at how parts of it have jettisoned everything distinctive about Quakerism and descended into a generic and intolerant Wesleyan fundamentalism. I am equally disappointed at two things. First, how other parts of Quaker preserved

FOREWORD

external features and rituals have become completely alienated from the key theological and spiritual insights of the first two hundred years of Quaker faith and practice. Second, that Quakers have abandoned the Christian substance of historical Quakerism. Tom falls into neither of these traps, and that is one of the things that I love about him, and that animates both his spiritual leadership among Friends and the ministry of producing these books.

My hope is that Quakers who read this will be challenged by his project—whether that means engaging other religious traditions with an uncomfortable openness and curiosity, or looking at the long spiritual and theological tradition of Christianity with an uncomfortable willingness to "come home," knowing that traditional Quakerism is not, and never has been, a foe of interreligious sympathy, curiosity, and collaboration.

Patrick J. Nugent

Patrick J. Nugent is President of the Dayton Performing Arts Alliance in Dayton, OH. He graduated with a degree in Latin, Greek, and theology from Xavier University. He has Master of Divinity and Ph.D. degrees from the Divinity School of the University of Chicago. He was on the faculty of religion at Earlham College and the founding Director of the Newlin Quaker Center there. He served as Principal and Associate Professor of Theology at Friends Theological College, Kaimosi, Kenya. He is a recorded minister in the New Association of Friends. After leaving academic life to help care for family members, he has been a fundraiser and executive in the social services and the arts, including service with the Annapolis Symphony Orchestra and Lyric Opera of Chicago before his current position. He and his wife, Mary Kay, have two adult biological children, a now-grown foster son. They are recreational sailors, lovers of music, Xavier basketball fans, and members of West Richmond Meeting of Friends in Indiana.

QUAKER BIBLE STUDY FOREWORD

My name is Francis Wayne and I am a Quaker and Maryknoll Lay Missioner working in Kenya. I started meeting with the Annapolis Friends for Bible study June 2023. We did six-week study sessions by Zoom. I became the host of the meetings, which means I keep the attendants on topic and I get to choose the scripture readings. For the first six-week session I chose Old Testament readings. We use the "Friendly Bible Study" method developed by Joanne and Larry Spears. The method is designed to compare the actions of our daily lives with the availability of continuing revelation of God through reading, contemplating, and discussing scripture, discovering the presence of God in our lives. That six-week course went really well.

The next Bible study began January 2024. By this time, I had read Thomas Wolfe & Companions' book "Thirty-Three Ways Seven Faiths Agree with Meher Baba." Thomas' book reminded me of the principles I have attained through prayer, contemplation, and reading a variety of scriptures, and practice daily in my life as a missioner. Because these principles are clearly defined in Scripture, I have a perception that I am "living the Gospel." Thomas' book also made the next six-week Bible study easy to plan: I had at hand thirty-three principles and their companion scripture to choose from for the six-week study. For January the study group and I followed "Section Three: Proper Effort," the first principle being "Do not shirk your responsibility." The companion scripture is 2 Corinthians 9.6-8 (AV), which verse six states "He which soweth sparingly shall reap also sparingly; and he which soweth bountifully shall reap bountifully." I find that if I read all Scripture, Old and New, always with the flavor of God's presence, I can imagine, even sometimes experience, God's presence in my actions. The method "Friendly Bible Study" guides the participant with questions like "What is the author's main point?" With this in mind I can relate that answer to the availability of God's presence in my life today. A general theme

QUAKER BIBLE STUDY FOREWORD

is "Love God always."

Thomas' book enhances relating by correlating principles with God's revelation. And there is a bonus: The book also correlates the same principles with the Scriptures of six other Faiths. I feel hope knowing that people everywhere are practicing the same principles because of God's presence in their lives also. Thanks TT (Tender Tom) & Companions for compiling this spiritual lesson.

Francis Wayne
Kenya (Maryknoll Lay Missioner)

INTRODUCTION FOR FRIENDS OF TRUTH QUAKERS

"That there is Universal Light, every age does testify. Not a nation in this world, nor an age throughout all time, has been left destitute of the discovery of Inner Light."

> William Penn
> *Sandy Foundation [of Christianity] Shaken,* 1668

For Orthodox Christian Quakers this book is a Guide to a Christian witness whose Testimonies do not exclude any Soul.

For Liberal (Hicksite) Quakers,* Christians, and those finding silence otherwise, this book serves as an educational guide to "where we all agree." Eighty-three percent of the world's population holds one of twelve faiths that agree with our Society's religious Testimonies.†

---

* Modern-day liberal Quakers are the Hicksite part of the orthodox Hicksite split. Elias Hicks did not like the label 'Hicksite.' He preferred 'Tolerants,' as opposed to 'Orthodox.'

† According to a Pew Institute religious survey done in 2004. Pew Institute surveys are considered to be the 'gold standard' of religious surveys.

INTRODUCTION

FOR FRIENDS
NOT YET "FRIENDS OF TRUTH"
(A/K/A QUAKERS*)

Friends with a capital "F" invite friends to join us in "Holy Experiment" by reading this book with an open heart.

The United States of America was born in 1776 out of the Holy Experiment of the Quakers in the Valley of Penn (William Penn) otherwise known as Pennsylvania. This "Holy Experiment" of the Quakers was based on God's Inner Light within each person, and a love-filled tolerance for all forms of worship, which came from "quietness and confidence"† born of silent worship. Does not our great country need a return to loving tolerance?

For those who do not yet know the Inner Light of Quaker Meetings, our offering *Thirty-three Ways Seven Faiths Agree with the Quakers* serves as a glimpse into the Religious Society of "Friends of Truth" currently known as the Quakers.

i

---

*   'Quaker' was a derogatory term that a Quaker-averse judge had come up with. He, very sarcastically, said, "You people quake before God." The Friends of Truth agreed and the term got adopted into popular culture.

†   Reference to *Isaiah* 30:15, which states "In quietness and confidence shall be our strength."

INTRODUCTION

TESTIMONIES FROM CHRIST'S SERMON ON THE MOUNT

The chapters in this book are organized using five Christian Quaker Testimonies that are taken from Jesus the Christ's Sermon on the Mount found in the Christian Good News according to Matthew in Chapters 5-9.

Peace
Equality
Simplicity
Truth in Integrity
Order in Community of God's Good News

"Tolerant" (Liberal or Hicksite) Friends of today have slightly different Testimonies. Along the way Tolerant Friends removed Truth and Order, and added Integrity, Community, and Stewardship to find Quaker Testimonies in

Simplicity
Peace
Integrity (instead of Truth)
Community (instead of Order in the Good News)
Equality
Stewardship

PREFACE

William Penn's Method and The Book Gift, 1997

I grew up Christian in the United Methodist Church and the Church of England. In fact, I was considering becoming clergy in the Church of England when I went to the University of Pennsylvania (UPenn). However, because of the Vietnam War, the fact that my family belonged to a military church, and the exclusiveness of the Christian creed, I could no longer self-identify as a Christian.

One day, at the rise of meeting at Adelphi Friends Monthly Meeting, a woman named Jane Furniss gave me *The Collected Works of William Penn*. It was a huge book, about 24x30 inches and 1,000 pages, and it was one of the original printings from 1728. She handed it to me and said, "I want you to have this because I know you're one of the few people who will actually read it."

So I sat right down in the sanctuary of Adelphi Friends Meeting and started reading. As God would have it, I opened right up to *The Sandy Foundation of Christianity Shaken*, which William Penn wrote when he was twenty-three years old. He printed 10,000 copies and distributed them throughout London at his own expense. What William Penn does in that small, thirty-page pamphlet is remove Christian exclusivity from the message that God's Light is within every person. Upon reading this pamphlet, I immediately, internally said to myself, "I can be a Christian by this definition because it doesn't exclude anybody." This epiphany was a huge moment because my inability to identify as a Christian had been painful for my family and me.

Back to William Penn: one week after publication and distribution of *The Sandy Foundation of Christianity Shaken*, Penn was condemned to death for heresy and imprisoned in the Tower of London for nine months. During that time, he wrote

PREFACE

No Cross, No Crown, in which he perfected his method of going through scripture and finding examples of the inward light in every person. Specifically, he examined the Tanakh, the Jewish scripture, and multiple Greek philosophers, and he found examples of about thirty principles where they agreed that the light of God is accessible to every heart directly.

Jane Furniss was right—I am one of those people who read *The Collected Works of William Penn* cover to cover, and I realized that William Penn had perfected this method, called the synoptic method, of finding commonalities in different scriptures. When you talk about the "Synoptic Gospels," it means the Gospels of Mark, Matthew, and Luke, because they agree with each other. What I see Be Friendly Ministries doing is illustrating how the scripture of different religions are synoptic. The synoptic good news (which is what "gospel" means) is now the whole world of scripture rather than just Judeo-Christian scripture. As I read about the method William Penn had perfected in his lifetime, it fit perfectly with the idea I had in Meherabad in 1988. Be Friendly Ministries combines the method of William Penn with the principles of Meher Baba to create a comprehensive understanding of the consistency of God's news. Amen and Hallelujah!

PREFACE

Maryland Council of Social Studies

After five years of laboring together with eleven faith communities, the Interfaith Conference (IFC) of Metropolitan D.C. published the *Teaching About Religion (T.A.R.) Handbook*. We subsequently published three supplements on the following topics—symbols of each faith community, what they teach about the environment, and each faith's values. These publications are available on the IFC of Metropolitan D.C.'s website—ifcmw.org.

We tested the *T.A.R. Handbook* in Virginia, and Fairfax County bought dozens of copies. So we decided to take it to the Maryland Council of Social Studies convention in October 2000. Coincidentally, the National Council of Social Studies was having their national convention in early December in Washington, D.C. However, we decided not to participate in that convention until we found out if the *T.A.R. Handbook* was well received by the Maryland social studies teachers.

At the conference of Maryland social studies teachers, we were amazed and pleased that virtually every social studies teacher rejoiced that someone had done this work. The primary reason the social studies teachers find this work valuable is because they don't have to study the religion to teach it, as well as because each religion vetted their own chapter; therefore, the answers to the forty-four questions are completely authentic and referenced. It is therefore very easy for the social studies teachers to share this information with their students because all they have to do is compile the lesson plans.

One possible future project would be to collect these lesson plans into a meta-analysis because many social studies teachers created lesson plans to teach world religions from the T.A.R. Handbook.

My favorite part of the story: at about noon, when we realized we had a hit and we had sold dozens of the *T.A.R. Handbook* to enthusiastic social studies teachers from Maryland, D.C., Rao, one of the Hindu IFC board members, turned to me and

PREFACE

said, "We really blew it."

Tom: "What do you mean we really blew it? We're getting incredible reception!"

D.C. Rao: "We really blew it by not signing up for the National Council of Social Studies Convention in early December."

I sadly agreed that it really should have gone to the national level, and the thought that it had to wait another year was disappointing.

The next person who walked into the booth was Susan Griffin, who recognized me.

She pointed at me and said, "You used to be on the board of William Penn House."

And I said, "Yes I did."

She said, "I am the Executive Director of the National Council of Social Studies teachers, and is there any way I can help you with this work?"

D.C. Rao turned to me and said, "Well, I guess we have to let God do His part in this work, too." We told Susan the story of how we had been shortsighted in not signing up for the National Council of Social Studies. Susan pulled out her phone, called her administrative assistant, got us a booth, and reduced the cost of the booth by half. It was an amazing God-incidence. It sends chills up and down my spine just remembering that moment.

PREFACE

Saudis at The State Department

In 2010 I received a phone call: "Mr. Wolfe, this is the State Department. Would you be willing to meet with a delegation from Saudi Arabia?"

I was convinced it was some friend of mine goofing on me, so I said, "Sure, I'm the President of the United States, I'll meet with you whenever you want. Ha ha ha."

The voice on the phone said, "No, Mr. Wolfe, this really is the State Department of the United States, and we want you to come downtown and meet with a delegation from Saudi Arabia that has asked for you and Imam Johari Abdul Malik specifically to meet with them."

It turns out that the Saudi educators had found out that we were teaching Islam in the public school system of the United States again, and they wanted to vet how we were teaching their religion. So Imam Johari Abdul Malik and I decided to go to speak to a delegation of eighteen men from the higher levels of education in the Kingdom of Saudi Arabia.

When the Jewish members of the IFC Board found out we were going to meet with the Saudi delegation, they insisted that we had to look at what the Saudis taught about Jews in their textbooks. I have to admit I was convinced the Jewish members of the IFC were overreacting, partially because a man I had met and admired, Cat Stevens, was being challenged as a representative singer for the annual IFC concert, which happens every November. Because of the Jewish board members' challenge to Cat Stevens (who had converted to Islam) singing at the concert, I believed they were probably overreacting to the textbooks of the Saudis.

Johari and I got copies of the textbooks, which were available online. We were shocked to see that the teaching of hatred from elementary school through high school was well documented both in Arabic and in English. Johari and I made twenty-five copies of the textbooks in both Arabic and English

PREFACE

and decided to confront the delegation from Saudi Arabia about the hatred of Jews and Christians in their textbooks. We decided to honor the ancient Quaker maxim, "It's easier to ask for forgiveness than permission," and we did not inform the State Department of our plan.

At our three-hour meeting at the State Department, I was the only person in the room who did not speak fluent Arabic. The State Department provided two interpreters, and Johari and I presented how we were teaching Islam in the public school system, which the Saudis celebrated. They were very pleased with the depth and accuracy with which we represented their religion in the *T.A.R. Handbook*. I also shared with them that William Penn was condemned to death for teaching, among other things, that the light of God was in Muslims in 1668. The Saudis were shocked and very pleasantly surprised that at least one denomination of Christianity did not exclude Islam from the light of God.

After an hour of celebrating with the Saudis about the chapter of Islam in the *T.A.R. Handbook*, we verbally challenged their teaching of hatred of Jews in their textbooks to the very young through young adults. The Saudis insisted that they loved Yehudi and that there wasn't a problem. We then pulled out the eighty-page document of the actual textbooks used in the Saudi educational system and gave each member of the delegation and the interpreters a copy. I felt concern for the State Department representative who, once he saw what we were doing, realized that there was a potential for conflict.

Over the next hour and a half to two hours, we had a vibrant and forthright dialogue with the Saudi educators concerning teaching about other religions and demonizing other religions. Imam Johari and I shared with them a *tafsir*, which is a scriptural analysis of the *Qur'an* that celebrated the Jewish prophets and clearly showed that the *Qur'an* teaches interfaith respect and a strong admiration for the Jewish prophets.

PREFACE

There were some amazing moments in that two-hour conversation. One of the amazing moments was when Imam Johari mentioned that the Jews keep the Sabbath. It became obvious after three references to the Jewish Sabbath that not a single Saudi in the room could conceive of the Jewish people keeping a holy day of rest and worship. Johari and I were stunned. Later we said it was like trying to explain snow to a desert dweller; the Saudis just couldn't conceive that the Jewish people had a Sabbath.

Both Johari and I got the sense in our prayer and reflection later that the educators from Saudi Arabia are not where the problem lies. We found the educators very comfortable and respectful with the concept of celebrating the many, many passages in the *Qur'an* that celebrate the Jewish faith and prophets. In fact, we had two subsequent meetings with the Saudi delegations. During the second meeting, we met with the two heads of the Qur'anic Memorization Society, which is an organization that has taught 160,000 undergraduates to memorize the *Qur'an*. These men can sing any *surah* (chapter) of the *Qur'an*. They sang a dozen different *surahs* that celebrate David, Moses, Abraham, Jacob, Ishmael, and Isaac. They sang these *surahs* with their entire heart and a big smile on their face. What we did during the second meeting made it even more obvious that the educators were willing to celebrate the Jewish faith and prophets.

Subsequently, I presented this story to the American Jewish Committee. On the way back from that presentation I realized I had to stop doing this work, because it was so stressful and hate-filled, and there needed to be a larger organization that provided support to people who choose to do this work. Interestingly enough, Imam Johari came to the same conclusion the same week, and we both stopped working with the *T.A.R. Handbook* project.

The interaction with the Saudi educators showed me how misunderstanding and misrepresentation are entrenched in comparative religion within our faith communities. In the case of the Saudis it is institutionalized into the education system and

PREFACE

not just isolated to the houses of worship. Now, years later, I am deeply struck by remembering the events of those three meetings with the Saudi educators. What William Penn and Meher Baba have made simply obvious will not be simply obvious as a blessing to those still influenced by the teaching of hatred.

The television program *60 Minutes* broadcast an interview of a five-year-old Saudi girl, and she was asked, "What do you think about Jews?"

She replied, "We should kill them all," which took the interviewer aback.

He then asked, "Why? Why would you say that?"

She said, "Well, we know from the *Qur'an* that the *Quimat* (Apocaplyse) won't come and we won't all go to heaven until all the Jews are dead."

PREFACE

The Unity of The Good News, 2001

In 2001, I was at work at my business, Smile Herb Shop, and I had an intuition to go home to my prayer gazebo for a message. In the five minutes it took me to get home, I felt more and more strongly that there was definitely a message. So I went out to the prayer gazebo; within an hour of prayer, there was this golden light, the most amazing thing, in the gazebo, and the message was very simple: "The unity of the good news has been restored." The message repeated three times. It was clear to me that my calling in life was to live up to that message and to help other people understand that, as William Penn says, "There is not a nation in this world nor an age throughout all time that has been destitute of the discovery of inward light."

While this was happening, my first wife Linda heard that there was a tornado watch but she decided not to disturb me. It was the first tornado watch in College Park in eighty-five years. We didn't think much of it until the next day when we went out and saw the destruction the tornado had wrought on College Park, which had happened simultaneously as I received the message: "The unity of the good news has been restored." I have no idea what to make of this combination of events, but that's what happened. From then on I knew that part of God's reality in my heart was that the unity of the good news had been restored.

PREFACE

Katherine Peck Story

I was in the Refectory at the Meher Spiritual Center in Myrtle Beach, South Carolina, doing one of my favorite activities. I discovered a cookbook called *The Quaker Baker*, and I love to bake for people, particularly in religious retreat settings. I had spent the previous day baking with a lovely woman named Katherine Peck. She had heard me discussing Be Friendly Ministries and saying we use the method of William Penn and thirty-three Principles of Meher Baba, and she let me know she was a Quaker. I said, "Aww, two Quakers in the kitchen." I added, "Well, I'm the Clerk of Ministry and Worship at Annapolis Friends Meeting."

She said, "Oh! I'm the Clerk of Ministry and Worship at Celo Friends Meeting in the mountains of North Carolina!"

I then said, "As you know, it has been a long time since unprogrammed Quakers have recorded ministry, and I have applied to embrace and possibly record my ministry at Annapolis Friends Meeting."

She then said, "Oh! As you know, Celo Friends Meeting is a member of Southern Appalachian Yearly Meeting, and Southern Appalachian Yearly Meeting has not recorded ministry for decades as well, and we just recorded our first minister, Geeta McGaughy, a medical doctor who is doing a ministry on the environment, a traveling ministry from Quaker meeting to Quaker meeting. Would you like me to send you the committee's minutes on how we recorded ministry for the first time in decades?"

It was just a coincidence, of course, that her committee had done the work that the Ministry and Worship Committee at Annapolis Friends Meeting was about to embark on. Then she said (it was her first visit to the Meher Center), "I am beginning to believe there might be something to this Meher Baba fellow."

PREFACE

The Al Nur Mosque

I am the co-chair of the Greater Annapolis Interfaith Network, and we have community programs on the second Thursday of every month. We had scheduled the Annapolis Immigration Justice Network (AIJN) to hold a program on the second Thursday of March 2019, which was the 15th. Understandably, given the horrific state of immigration policy, AIJN was overwhelmed and had to cancel their scheduled program at the last minute.

So I decided, on the spur of the moment, to do a program about "The Unity of the Good News." It was a delightful sharing, and I again felt God's guidance and loving hand in this ministry.

The next morning during a business meeting, my administrative assistant asked me if I knew what had happened in New Zealand. She shared with me the horrible murder of fifty-one Muslims at the Al Nur Mosque and Linwood Islamic Center that

Al-Nur Mosque, Christchurch, New Zealand

PREFACE

had happened the day before. We shared a few tears and then held our business meeting.

The next morning during my prayer and meditation time, the question kept coming up: "What time was it in Christchurch, New Zealand, when the incident occurred?" Three times this question came up.

New Zealand is eighteen hours ahead of Eastern Standard Time. When preparations began for our program at 6:30 pm EST, it was 2:30 pm in New Zealand, which was exactly the height of the intensity of the assault on the two mosques.

My heart knew this was not a coincidence, and I again felt God's *nazar* (loving gaze and guidance) on this ministry. Friends, it was the same moment in time that the extreme nature of the problem presented itself, as well as the solution.

PREFACE

Unity of Good News Restored, 2020

An attorney friend and I were having a delightful dinner in an upscale restaurant in Myrtle Beach, South Carolina. I was describing with enthusiasm the momentum that Be Friendly Ministries was gathering within the Quaker and Meher Baba communities to show God's faithfulness and consistency over the past 4,000 years.

Our waiter William, coming and going, approached the table: "May I ask you a question about religion?"

"Sure," I said, aware that this does not usually happen in the middle of fine dining.

William said, "My pastor says Muhammad is sent from Satan. Do you believe Muhammad is sent from the Devil?"

I shared with William the story of my mother's funeral, during which the United Methodist clergyman and I stood in two pulpits and shared fourteen praises of Jesus, each one followed by the other pulpit exclaiming in celebration: " Isn't scripture wonderful!" After fourteen praises of Jesus, I praised one last time, "Isn't scripture wonderful!"

William was as surprised as my conservative Christian relatives from North Carolina to hear that all of the fourteen praises of Jesus came from the *Qur'an*. He asked that I send him the fourteen quotes praising Jesus from the *Qur'an*; I offered instead to send him a draft of a planned booklet from Be Friendly Ministries, *Thirty-Three Ways Muhammad Agrees with Jesus*.

We were the last diners to leave the restaurant, and William shared with us his humble knowing: "It just doesn't make sense to me that hundreds of millions of people are following Satan." My beloved wife called it to my attention and my heart was struck by the fact that often the laity is wiser about separation than the clergy.

PREFACE

SECTION ONE

PEACE

> For Earth he asks it: the full joy of Heaven
>   Knoweth no change of waning or increase;
> The great heart of the Infinite beats even,
>   Untroubled flows the river of his peace.

John Greenleaf Whittier, "Worship," in *The Complete Poetical Works of John Greenleaf Whittier*, (Middletown, DE: Forgotten Books, 2012), p 123-124.

PEACE PRINCIPLE 1

PEACE OF MIND

If you have the peace of a frozen lake, then too you will realize Me.

Quakers:

"...& Soe keep low at the bottome, that the tree which cannot bring forth evill fruite, may take roott downeward & upward, that soe thy growth may be true, rooted & grounded into the rocke, unmoveable, that the stormes & tempests cannot beate downe, that when troubles & tryalls & afflictions comes, thou may know A sure habitation, & portion, & liveing strength in the Lord[,] & A pure peace which cannot be taken from thee...".

Margaret Fell, *Undaunted Zeal: The Letters of Margaret Fell.* Edited by Elsa F. Glines. (Richmond, Indiana: Friends United Press, 2003) "To Colonel William Osburne 1657," p. 241.

"...showing, as the way opened, that where people were truly humble, used themselves to business, and were content with a plain way of life, that it had ever been attended with more true peace and calmness of mind than those have had who, aspiring to greatness and outward show, have grasped hard for an income to support themselves in it."

John Woolman, *The Journal and Major Essays of John Woolman.* Edited by Phillips P. Moulton. (Richmond, Indiana: Friends United Press, 2007), p. 114-115.

PEACE TESTIMONY 1

Jesus:

"Peace I leave with you, my peace I give unto you: not as the world giveth, give I unto you. Let not your heart be troubled, neither let it be afraid."

Authorized (King James) Version (AV). (Nashville, TN: Thomas Nelson, 2016), John 14:27.

Tanakh:

For thus said my Lord God,
The Holy One of Israel,
"You shall triumph by stillness and quiet;
Your victory shall come about
Through calm and confidence."

Tanakh: The Holy Scriptures, New JPS Translation. (Jerusalem: The Jewish Publication Society, 1985), Isaiah 30:15.

I am ever mindful of the Lord's presence;
       He is at my right hand; I shall never be shaken.
So my heart rejoices,
       my whole being exults,
       and my body rests secure.

Tanakh: The Holy Scriptures. Psalms 16:8–9.

1. PEACE OF MIND

Zarathushtra:

Thou art Divine, I know, O Lord Supreme,
Since Good found entrance to my heart through Love,
This taught me that for steady inner growth
Quiet and silent meditation's best.

Irach J.S. Taraporewala, *The Divine Songs of Zarathushtra*, 3rd edition. (Mumbai, India: Hukhta Foundation, 2014), Ustavaiti 1.15—Yasna 43.15.

Krishna:

Indifferent to scriptures, your mind
stands by itself, unmoving,
absorbed in deep meditation.
This is the essence of yoga.

Bhagavad Gita. Translated by Stephen Mitchell. (New York, NY: Three Rivers Press, 2000), 2.53.

The man whom desires enter
as rivers flow into the sea,
filled yet always unmoving—
that man finds perfect peace.

Bhagavad Gita. 2.70.

Buddha:

Wise people, after they have listened to the laws, become serene like a deep, clear and still lake.

The Dhammapada. Translated by Irving Babbitt. (New York, NY: New Directions Books, 1965), 6:82.

Even though a speech be composed of a thousand words, but words without sense, one word of sense is better, which if a man hears he becomes quiet. Even though a stanza be composed of a thousand words but words without sense, one word of a stanza is better which if a man hears, he becomes quiet. Though a man recite a hundred stanzas made up of senseless words, one word of the Law is better, which if a man hears, he becomes quiet.

The Dhammapada. 8:100–102.

Muhammad's Revelation:[*]

"... Behold, it shall be a sign of his [rightful] dominion that you will be granted a heart endowed by your Sustainer with inner peace and with all that is enduring."

i

---

[*] It is important to know that in Islamic belief, Muhammad did not write the Holy Qur'an, he transcribed it from visions given to him by Allah through the angel Gabriel. In other faith traditions, we may refer to the Prophet as being the author of a scriptural quote. For Islam, however, we refer to "Muhammad's Revelation" rather than Muhammad himself. This is an essential distinction in the way that Islam views the difference between Allah and the Prophet Muhammad and can help us understand some of the key theological arguments between Islam and Christianity

1. PEACE OF MIND

The Qur'an. Translated and explained by Muhammad Asad. (London, England: The Book Foundation, 2003), Al-Baqarah (The Cow) 2:248.

But those who shall have attained to faith and done righteous deeds will be brought into gardens through which running waters flow, therein to abide by their Sustainer's leave, and will be welcomed with the greeting, "Peace!"

The Qur'an. Ibrahim (Abraham) 14:23.

Meher Baba:

Realization of the unity of all is accompanied by peace and unfathomable bliss.

Meher Baba, *Discourses*, 7th edition. (North Myrtle Beach, SC: Sheriar Foundation, 1987), p. 14.

Selfness for all brings about undisturbed harmony without loss of discrimination, and unshakable peace without indifference to the surroundings.

Meher Baba, *Discourses*, 7th edition. p. 14.

PEACE TESTIMONY 1

**All as God wills, who wisely heeds
To give or to withhold,
And knoweth more of all my needs
Than all my prayers have told.**

John Greenleaf Whittier, "My Psalm," in *The Complete Poetical Works of John Greenleaf Whittier*, p 242-243.

PEACE PRINCIPLE 2

REAL SURRENDER IS RESIGNATION TO THE WILL OF GOD

The only Real Surrender is that in which poise is undisturbed by any adverse circumstance, and the individual, amidst every kind of hardship, is resigned with perfect calm to the will of God.

Quakers:

"For whenever the Lord suffers his enemyes to exercise their Cruelty upon his Children & servents it is for the Accomplishing of his owne will & pleasure, which is for his owne service; And therefore dear harts be not weary, for when the Lords end and time is come then will deliverance come. For in vaine is it looked for, from the hills and from the Mountaines but from the Lord alone in whom is everlasting strength."

Margaret Fell, *Undaunted Zeal: The Letters of Margaret Fell*, "To Alexander Parker and George Whitehead July 24, 1660," p. 287.

This people [Quakers] insists that Chrisitianity teaches people to beat their swords into plowshares and their spears into pruning hooks and never again to train for war. They not only refused to take revenge for injuries received, condemning it as unchristian, but they freely forgave those who had been cruel to them—even when vengeance was within their power. Many notable examples of their efforts to overcome injustice and oppression could be provided.

William Penn, *Twenty-First Century Penn: Writings on the Faith and Practice of the People Called Quakers*, 1694. (Richmond, Indiana: Earlham School of Religion Press, 2003), p. 364.

2. REAL SURRENDER TO THE WILL OF GOD

"And being clearly convinced in my judgment that to place my whole trust in God was best for me, I felt renewed engagements that in all things I might act on an inward principle of virtue and pursue worldly business no further than as Truth opened my way therein."

John Woolman, *The Journal and Major Essays of John Woolman*, p 32.

Jesus:

"Not every one that saith unto me, Lord, Lord, shall enter into the kingdom of heaven; but he that doeth the will of my Father which is in heaven."

Matthew 7:21 (AV).

Tanakh:

When you pass through water,
I will be with you;
Through streams,
They shall not overwhelm you.
When you walk through fire,
You shall not be scorched;
Through flame,
It shall not burn you.
For I the Lord am your God,
The Holy One of Israel, your Savior.

Tanakh: The Holy Scriptures. Isaiah 43:2–3.

PEACE TESTIMONY 2

But ask the beasts, and they will teach you;
The birds of the sky, they will tell you,
Or speak to the earth, it will teach you;

The fish of the sea, they will inform you.
Who among all these does not know
That the hand of the Lord has done this?
In His hand is every living soul
And the breath of all mankind.

Tanakh: The Holy Scriptures. Job 12:7-10.

Zarathushtra:

O Wise Follower of God, I have taught
That action, not inaction, higher stands,
Obeying, then, His Will, worship through deeds;
The Great Lord, wondrous Guardian of the Worlds,
Through His Eternal Law discriminates,
Who are the truly Wise and who Unwise.

The Divine Songs of Zarathushtra. Ustavaiti 4.17—Yasna 46.17.

Krishna:

Surrendering all thoughts of outcome,
unperturbed, self-reliant,
he does nothing at all, even
when fully engaged in actions.

Bhagavad Gita. 4.20.

2. REAL SURRENDER TO THE WILL OF GOD

The resolute in yoga surrender
results, and gain perfect peace;
the irresolute, attached to results,
are bound by everything they do.

Bhagavad Gita. 5.12.

Buddha:

Good people walk on, whatever befall; the good do not prattle, longing for pleasure; whether touched by happiness or sorrow, wise people never appear elated or depressed.

The Dhammapada. 6:83.

Muhammad's Revelation:

O you who have attained to faith! Seek aid in steadfast patience and prayer: for, behold, God is with those who are patient in adversity.... And most certainly shall We try you by means of danger, and hunger, and loss of worldly goods, of lives and of [labour's] fruits. But give glad tidings unto those who are patient in adversity – who, when calamity befalls them, say, "Verily, unto God do we belong and, verily, unto Him we shall return."

The Qur'an. Al-Baqarah (The Cow) 2:153–156.

"Hence, we shall certainly bear with patience whatever hurt you may do us: for, all who have trust [in His existence] must place their trust in God [alone]!"

The Qur'an. 'Ibrāhīm (Abraham) 14:12.

Thus, [O Prophet,] if they argue with thee, say, "I have surrendered my whole being unto God, and [so have] all who follow me!" — and ask those who have been vouchsafed revelation aforetime, as well as all unlettered people, "Have you [too] surrendered yourselves unto Him?" And if they surrender themselves unto Him, they are on the right path; but if they turn away — behold, thy duty is no more than to deliver the message: for God sees all that is in [the hearts of] His creatures.

The Qur'an. Al-Imran (The House of Imran) 3:20.

Meher Baba:
Wanting is a state of disturbed equilibrium of mind, and nonwanting is a state of stable poise. The poise of nonwanting can only be maintained by an unceasing disentanglement from all stimuli—whether pleasant or painful, agreeable or disagreeable. In order to remain unmoved by the joys and sorrows of this world, the mind must be completely detached from the external and internal stimuli.

Meher Baba, *Discourses*, 7th edition. P. 46.

Angel of Patience! set to calm
Our feverish brows with cooling palm;
To lay the storms of hope and fear,
And reconcile life's smile and tear;
The throbs of wounded pride to still
And make our own our Father's will!

O thou who mournest on thy way,
With longings for the close of day;
He walks with thee, that Angel kind,
And gently whispers, "Be resigned:
Bear up, bear on, the end shall tell
The dear Lord ordereth all things well!"

John Greenleaf Whittier, "The Angel of Patience," in *The Complete Poetical Works of John Greenleaf Whittier*, p 96.

PEACE PRINCIPLE 3

PELOVE IS PATIENCE AND CONTENTMENT

If we endure our lot with patience and contentment, accepting it as His Will, we are loving God.

Quakers:

"— For if you walk in the Light, and abide in the Light, which is Low and Meek, and wait in Silence and Faithfulness, and Obedience, wait Patiently, and you shall have the Light of Life."

Margaret Fell, *Undaunted Zeal: The Letters of Margaret Fell*, "An Epistle to Friends 1653," p. 52.

We must have patience for should the first lesson contain everything? Students who are willing to learn and who listen to and follow the directions of a capable teacher will grow in knowledge. If they do not attend to the master, their failure to learn should be laid at their feet, not the teachers. Consider this from the gospel of John: "if you do my will, you will learn more of my doctrine."

William Penn, *Twenty-First Century Penn*, "The Christian Quaker," 1674. P. 98.

Jesus:

Cast not away therefore your confidence, which hath great recompense of reward. For ye have need of patience, that, after ye have done the will of God, ye might receive the promise.

Hebrews 10:35–36 (AV).

3. LOVE IS PATIENCE AND CONTENTMENT

Tanakh:

Leave all to the Lord;
    trust in Him; He will do it.
He will cause your vindication to shine forth like the light,
    the justice of your case, like the noonday sun.
Be patient and wait for the Lord,
    do not be vexed by the prospering man
    who carries out his schemes.

Tanakh: The Holy Scriptures. Psalms 37:5-7.

The LORD is good to those who trust in Him,
To the one who seeks Him;
It is good to wait patiently
Till rescue comes from the Lord.
It is good for a man, when young,
To bear a yoke;
Let him sit alone and be patient,
When He has laid it upon him.
Let him put his mouth to the dust—
There may yet be hope.
Let him offer his cheek to the smiter;
Let him be surfeited with mockery.
For the Lord does not
Reject forever,
But first afflicts, then pardons
In His abundant kindness.

Tanakh: The Holy Scriptures. Lamentations 3: 25-32.

Zarathushtra:

That I the better way might choose, reveal,
        What in accord with Truth Thou hast ordained;
Reveal to me through Love, through Love,
        That I might be uplifted and be sure,
Whatever comes at Thy Command is best
        For me—whether reward or otherwise.

The Divine Songs of Zarathushtra. Ahunavaiti 4.5—Yasna 31.5.

Krishna:

When a man gives up all desires
that emerge from the mind, and rests
contented in the Self by the Self,
he is called a man of firm wisdom.

Bhagavad Gita. 2.55.

Buddha:

Patience, long-suffering, is the highest form of penance, Nirvana the highest of all things, say the Awakened; for he is not an anchorite who strikes another, he is not an ascetic who insults another.

The Dhammapada. 14:184.

3. LOVE IS PATIENCE AND CONTENTMENT

Muhammad's Revelation:

Verily, in this [reminder] there are messages indeed for all who are wholly patient in adversity and deeply grateful [to God]. The Qur'an. ʾIbrāhīm (Abraham) 14:5.

Clearly, indeed, have We spelled out these messages unto people who [are willing to] take them to heart! Theirs shall be an abode of peace with their Sustainer; and He shall be near unto them in result of what they have been doing.

The Qur'an. Al-An ʿām (Cattle) 6:126–127.

Meher Baba:

...one of the first requirements of the aspirant is that he should combine unfailing enthusiasm with unyielding patience. Once an individual is determined to realize the Truth, he finds that his path is beset with many difficulties, and there are very few who persist with steady courage till the very end. It is easy to give up the effort when one is confronted with obstacles.

Meher Baba, *Discourses*, 7th edition. P. 355-356.

PEACE TESTIMONY 3

If man becomes desireless and contented, he will be free from his self-inflicted suffering. His imagination will not be constantly harassed by feverish reaching out toward things that really do not matter, and he will be established in unassailable peace. When an individual is thus contented, he does not require any solutions to problems, because the problems that confront worldly persons have disappeared. He has no problems, therefore he does not have to worry about their solution. For him the complexities of life do not exist because his life becomes utterly simple in the state of desirelessness.

Meher Baba, *Discourses*, 7th edition. P. 394.

Once, on the errands of his mercy bent,
Buddha, the holy and benevolent,
Met a fell monster, huge and fierce of look,
Whose awful voice the hills and forests shook.
"O son of peace!" the giant cried, "thy fate
Is sealed at last, and love shall yield to hate."
The unarmed Buddha looking, with no trace
Of fear or anger, in the monster's face,
In pity said : "Poor fiend, even thee I love."
Lo! as he spake the sky-tall terror sank
To hand-breadth size ; the huge abhorrence shrank
Into the form and fashion of a dove;
And where the thunder of its rage was heard,
Circling above him sweetly sang the bird:
"Hate hath no harm for love," so ran the song;
"And peace unweaponed conquers every wrong!"

John Greenleaf Whittier, "Disarmament," in *The Complete Poetical Works of John Greenleaf Whittier*, p 374.

PEACE PRINCIPLE 4

LOVE IS DOING NO HARM

If we understand and feel that the greatest act of devotion and worship to God is not to hurt or harm any of His beings, we are loving God.

Quakers:

...he increasing faith that true principles are capable of being applied now, and that it is no visionary idea that the "sword may be beaten into the ploughshare and the spear into the pruning hook," that "nation shall not lift up sword against nation, neither shall they learn war anymore" — these all give evidence that "the kingdom of God is at hand," when "violence shall no more be heard in the land, wasting and destruction within her borders.

Lucretia Mott, *Lucretia Mott Speaks: The Essential Speeches and Sermons*, "Sermon to the Medical Students, 1849." (Chicago, Illinois: University of Illinois Press, 2017), p. 54.

They urge all to turn their zeal loose on sin and no longer to make war against each other. All wars and fightings arise in human covetousness not from the meek Spirit of Christ Jesus. Christ is the captain of a different warfare carried out with different weapons. Just as swearing gave way to speaking Truth, fighting gave way to faith and truth as Quaker doctrines and practices.

William Penn, *Twenty-First Century Penn*, "Rise and Progress of the People Called Quakers," 1694. P. 365.

4. LOVE IS DOING NO HARM

Jesus:

"But I say unto you, Love your enemies, bless them that curse you, do good to them that hate you, and pray for them which despitefully use you, and persecute you; That ye may be the children of your Father which is in heaven; for he maketh his sun to rise on the evil and on the good, and sendeth rain on the just and on the unjust."

Matthew 5:44–45 (AV).

Tanakh:

Do not devise harm against your fellow
Who lives trustfully with you.

Tanakh: The Holy Scriptures. Proverbs 3:29.

The wolf and the lamb shall graze together,
And the lion shall eat straw like the ox,
And the serpent's food shall be earth.
In all My sacred mount
Nothing evil or vile shall be done
—said the Lord.

Tanakh: The Holy Scriptures. Isaiah 65:25.

Zarathushtra:

Keep Hatred far from you; let nothing tempt
Your minds to violence:—hold on to Love.

The Divine Songs of Zarathushtra. Spenta-Mainyu 2.7—Yasna 48.7.

Krishna:

Knowing that it is eternal,
unborn, beyond destruction,
how could you ever kill?
And whom could you kill, Arjuna?

Bhagavad Gita. 2.21.

He who neither disturbs
the world nor is disturbed by it,
who is free of all joy, fear, envy—
that man is the one I love best.

Bhagavad Gita. 12.15.

Buddha:

He who, seeking his own happiness, does not injure or kill beings who also long for happiness, will find happiness after death.

The Dhammapada. 10:132.

4. LOVE IS DOING NO HARM

He who, though richly adorned, exercises tranquility, is quiet, subdued, restrained, chaste, and has ceased to injure all other beings, is indeed Brahman, an ascetic, a friar.

The Dhammapada. 10:142.

What now is Right Action? There someone avoids the killing of living beings, and abstains from it. Without stick or sword, conscientious, full of sympathy, he is anxious for the welfare of all living beings.

A Buddhist Bible. Edited by Dwight Goddard. (Boston, MA: Beacon Press, 1970), p. 44.

Muhammad's Revelation:

And do not take any human being's life – [the life] which God has willed to be sacred – otherwise than in [the pursuit of] justice. Hence, if anyone has been slain wrongfully, We have empowered the defender of his rights [to exact a just retribution]; but even so, let him not exceed the bounds of equity in [retributive] killing. [And as for him who has been slain wrongfully –] behold, he is indeed succoured [by God]!

The Qur'an. Al-ʾIsrāaʾ (The Night Journey) 17:32–33.

PEACE TESTIMONY 4

Meher Baba:

Nonviolence pure and simple means love infinite. It is the goal of life. When this state of pure divine love is reached, the aspirant is at one with God. To reach this goal there must be intense longing, and the aspirant who has this longing to realize the supreme state has to begin by practicing what is termed nonviolence of the brave. This applies to those who, though not one with all through actual Realization, consider no one as their enemy. They try to win over even the aggressor through love and give up their lives if attacked, not through fear but through love.

Meher Baba, *Discourses*, 7th edition. P. 73.

O thou who mournest on thy way,
With longings for the close of day;
He walks with thee, that Angel kind,
And gently whispers, "Be resigned:
Bear up, bear on, the end shall tell
The dear Lord ordereth all things well!"

John Greenleaf Whittier, "The Angel of Patience," in *The Complete Poetical Works of John Greenleaf Whittier*, p 96.

PEACE PRINCIPLE 5

ACCEPT HAPPINESS AND SUFFERING WITH EQUAL POISE

When you feel happy, think: "God wants me to be happy."
When you suffer, think: "God wants me to suffer."

Quakers:

"I feel there [are?] very many passing middle age of life who are suffering themselves, and their own power for good, to become dwarfed by expecting too much, looking for too high an evidence, for more than has been granted, not having sufficient faith to accept what has been given and obey it, and trust in the assurance that to be faithful thus in the little, will be an opening into that which is greater."

Lucretia Mott, *Lucretia Mott Speaks: The Essential Speeches and Sermons*, "Philadelphia Quarterly Meeting, Race Street, November 4, 1873," p. 206.

"The Most High doth not often speak with an outward voice to our outward ears, but if we humbly meditate on his perfections, consider that he is perfect wisdom and goodness and to afflict his creatures to no purpose would be utterly reverse to his nature, we shall hear and understand his language, both in his gentle and more heavy chastisements, and take heed that we do not in the wisdom of this world endeavour to escape his hand by means too powerful for us."

John Woolman, *The Journal and Major Essays of John Woolman*, p 105.

5. ACCEPT HAPPINESS AND SUFFERING WITH EQUAL POISE

Jesus:

We are troubled on every side, yet not distressed; we are perplexed, but not in despair; Persecuted, but not forsaken; cast down, but not destroyed.

2 *Corinthians* 4:8–9 (AV).

But seek ye first the kingdom of God, and his righteousness; and all these things shall be added unto you. Take therefore no thought for the morrow; for the morrow shall take thought for the things of itself. Sufficient unto the day is the evil thereof."

Matthew 6:33–34 (AV).

Tanakh:

See how happy is the man whom God reproves;
Do not reject the discipline of the Almighty.
He injures, but He binds up;
He wounds, but His hands heal.
He will deliver you from six troubles;
In seven no harm will reach you:
In famine He will redeem you from death,
In war, from the sword.

Tanakh: The Holy Scriptures. Job 5:17–20.

Consider God's doing! Who can straighten what He has twisted? So in a time of good fortune enjoy the good fortune; and in a time of misfortune, reflect: The one no less than the other was God's doing; consequently, man may find no fault with Him.

Tanakh: The Holy Scriptures. Ecclesiastes 7:13-14.

Zarathushtra:

I ask, God, that I learn from Thee,
>How Fate has come upon us, and shall come;

What silent yearnings of good men and true
>Have been recorded in the Book of Life,

What yearnings, too, that follow the Untruth;
>How do these stand, when the account is closed?

The Divine Songs of Zarathushtra. Ahunavaiti 4.14—Yasna 31.14.

Krishna:

He whose mind is untroubled
by any misfortune, whose craving
for pleasures has disappeared,
who is free from greed, fear, anger,

who is unattached to all things,
who neither grieves nor rejoices
if good or if bad things happen—
that man is a man of firm wisdom.

Bhagavad Gita. 2.56–57.

...quiet, filled with devotion,
content with whatever happens,
at home wherever he is—
that man is the one I love best.

Bhagavad Gita. 12.19.

5. ACCEPT HAPPINESS AND SUFFERING WITH EQUAL POISE

Buddha:

Good people walk on, whatever befall; the good do not prattle, longing for pleasure; whether touched by happiness or sorrow, wise people never appear elated or depressed.

The Dhammapada. 6:83.

Just as a rock of one solid mass remains unshaken by the wind, even so, neither forms, nor sounds, nor odours, nor tastes, nor contacts of any kind, neither the desired nor the undesired, can cause such an [sic] one to waver. Steadfast is his mind, gained is deliverance.

A Buddhist Bible. P. 32.

Muhammad's Revelation:

[But] do you think that you could enter paradise without having suffered like those [believers] who passed away before you? Misfortune and hardship befell them, and so shaken were they that the apostle, and the believers with him, would exclaim, "When will God's succor come?" Oh, verily, God's succour is [always] near!

The Qur'an. Al-Baqarah (The Cow) 2:214.

And neither allow thy hand to remain shackled to thy neck, nor stretch it forth to the utmost limit [of thy capacity], lest thou find thyself blamed [by thy dependents], or even destitute. Behold, thy Sustainer grants abundant sustenance, or gives it in scant measure, unto whomever He wills: verily, fully aware is He of [the needs of] His creatures, and sees them all.

The Qur'an. Al-Israa (The Night Journey) 17:29-30.

Meher Baba:

It is your right to be happy, and yet you create your own unhappiness by wanting things. Wanting is the source of perpetual restlessness. If you do not get the thing you want, you are disappointed. And if you get it, you want more and more of it and become unhappy. Say "I do not want anything" and be happy. The continuous realization of the futility of wants will eventually lead you to Knowledge. This Self-knowledge will give you the freedom from wants that leads to the road to abiding happiness.

Meher Baba, *Discourses*, 7th edition. P. 12

Serving the Master is a joy for the disciple, even when it means an ordeal that tries his body or mind. Service offered under conditions of discomfort or inconvenience is a test of the disciple's devotion. The more trying such service becomes, the more welcome it is for the disciple. And as he voluntarily accepts physical and mental suffering in his devoted service to the Master, he experiences the bliss of spiritual fulfillment.

Meher Baba, *Discourses*, 7th edition. P. 150

O Love! O Life! Our faith and sight
    Thy presence maketh one:
As through transfigured clouds of white
    We trace the noon-day sun.

So, to our mortal eyes subdned,
    Flesh-veiled, but not concealed.
We know in thee the fatherhood
    And heart of God revealed.

We faintly hear, we dimly see,
    In differing phrase we pray;
But, dim or clear, we own in thee
    The Light, the Truth, the Way!

John Greenleaf Whittier, "Our Master," in *The Complete Poetical Works of John Greenleaf Whittier*, p 319-321.

PEACE PRINCIPLE 6

LOVING WITHOUT WANTING ANYTHING IN RETURN

If you have that love for Me that Saint Francis had for Jesus, then not only will you realize Me but you will please Me.

Quakers:

"...for God is Love, & he that dwells in God dwells in Love[,] & love is the fullfilling of the Law[,] & Love thinketh noe Evill nor doeth noe Evill, but overcometh Evill with good[,] & they that are endowed with this spirit of Love, are blessed of God...".

Margaret Fell, *Undaunted Zeal: The Letters of Margaret Fell,* "To King Charles II August ? 1660," p. 296.

"The natural mind is active about the things of this life, and in this natural activity business is proposed and a will in us to go forward in it. And as long as this natural will remains unsubjected, so long as there remains an obstruction against the clearness of divine light operating in us; but when we love God with all our heart and with all our strength, then in this love we love our neighbours as ourselves, and a tenderness of heart is felt toward all people...".

John Woolman, *The Journal and Major Essays of John Woolman,* p 177.

6. LOVING WITHOUT WANTING ANYTHING IN RETURN

Jesus:

And we have known and believed the love that God hath to us. God is love; and he that dwelleth in love dwelleth in God, and God in him. Herein is our love made perfect, that we may have boldness in the day of judgment: because as he is, so are we in this world. There is no fear in love; but perfect love casteth out fear: because fear hath torment. He that feareth is not made perfect in love. We love him, because he first loved us.

1 *John* 4:16-19 (KJV).

Love is patient; love is kind; love is not envious or boastful or arrogant or rude. It does not insist on its own way; it is not irritable or resentful; it does not rejoice in wrongdoing, but rejoices in the truth. It bears all things, believes all things, hopes all things, endures all things. Love never ends....And now faith, hope, and love abide, these three; and the greatest of these is love.

New Revised Standard Version Bible (NRSV). (Grand Rapids, MI: Zondervan Publishing House, 1989), 1 Corinthians 13:4-13.

Tanakh:

Then the Lord your God will open up your heart and the hearts of your offspring to love the Lord your God with all your heart and soul, in order that you may live... For the Lord will again delight in your well being.

Tanakh: The Holy Scriptures. Deuteronomy 30:6, 9.

Those who love me I love,
And those who seek me will find me...
My fruit is better than gold, fine gold,
And my produce better than choice silver...
I endow those who love me with substance.

Tanakh: The Holy Scriptures. Proverbs 8:17, 19, 21.

Zarathushtra:

With chants that well up from my Inmost Heart,
With hands uplifted, God, I beseech,
    That I, Thy humble Lover, Thee attain,
        Come closer unto Thee through Knowledge's help,
        Through Love's wonder-working Love.

The Divine Songs of Zarathushtra. Spenta-Mainyu 4.8—Yasna 50.8.

Krishna:

Even the heartless criminal,
if he loves me with all his heart,
will certainly grow into sainthood
as he moves toward me on this path.

Bhagavad Gita. 9.30.

6. LOVING WITHOUT WANTING ANYTHING IN RETURN

All those who love and trust me,
even the lowest of the low—
prostitutes, beggars, slaves—
will attain the ultimate goal.

Bhagavad Gita. 9.32.

Buddha:

The true Samana, he who is seeking the way to the Brahma World, lets his mind pervade all quarters of the world with thoughts of Love; first one quarter then the second quarter, then the third quarter and so the fourth quarter. And thus the whole wide world, above, below, around, and everywhere, does he continue to pervade with thoughts of love, far-reaching, beyond measure, all-embracing.

A Buddhist Bible. P. 71.

Muhammad's Revelation:

And [thus it was that Jesus always said], "Verily, God is my Sustainer as well as your Sustainer; so worship [none but] Him: this [alone] is a straight way."

The Qur'an. Marayam (Mary) 19:36.

And thereupon We caused [other of] Our apostles to follow in their footsteps; and [in the course of time] We caused them to be followed by Jesus, the son of Mary, upon whom We bestowed the Gospel; and in the hearts of those who [truly] followed him We engendered compassion and mercy. But as for monastic asceticism – We did not enjoin it upon them: they invented it themselves out of a desire for God's goodly acceptance. But then, they did not [always] observe it as it ought to have been observed: and so We granted their recompense unto such of them as had [truly] attained to faith, whereas many of them became iniquitous.

The Qur'an. Al-Hadid (Iron) 57:27.

Meher Baba:

Love is therefore rightly regarded as being the most important avenue leading to the realization of the Highest. In love the soul is completely absorbed in the Beloved and is therefore detached from the actions of the body or mind.

Meher Baba, *Discourses*, 7th edition. P. 54.

Through the intensity of this ever growing love, he eventually breaks through the shackles of the self and becomes united with the Beloved. This is the consummation of love. When love has thus found its fruition, it has become divine.

Meher Baba, *Discourses*, 7th edition. P. 115.

There is no sadhana [practice, striving, endeavor; directing toward the goal] greater than love, there is no law higher than love, and there is no goal that is beyond love—for love in its divine state becomes infinite. God and love are identical, and one who has divine love already has God.

Meher Baba, *Discourses*, 7th edition. P. 264.

SECTION TWO

EQUALITY

Whereby, while differing in degree
As finite from infinity,
The pain and loss for others borne,
Love's crown of suffering meekly worn,
The life man giveth for his friend
Becomes vicarious in the end;
Their healing place in nature take,
And make life sweeter for their sake.

John Greenleaf Whittier, "Miriam," in *The Complete Poetical Works of John Greenleaf Whittier*, p 341-347.

EQUALITY PRINCIPLE 1

SELF-SACRIFICE

The only Real Sacrifice is that in which, in pursuance of this Love, all things, body, mind, position, welfare, and even life itself are sacrificed.

Quakers:

"...And soe thinke it not strange concerning the firey tryall that is to try you[,] but rejoyce in as much as yee are made partakers of christs sufferings, and if you be reproached for the name of christ[,] happy are yee for therein the spirit of glory and of power resteth upon you, and in this ye have a cloud of witnesses [Heb. 12:1] and therin hath unity with all the saints in Light... and soe cast your care upon the Lord of heaven and earth for he careth for you, give up freely unto his good will and pleasure...".

Margaret Fell, *Undaunted Zeal: The Letters of Margaret Fell*, "To All Prisoners, From Lancaster Prison January 11, 1665," p. 389.

"And I have felt a renewed confirmation in the time of this voyage that the Lord in infinite love is calling to his visited children to so give up all outward possessions and means of getting treasures that his Holy Spirit may have free course in their hearts and direct them in all their proceedings. To feel the substance pointed at in this figure, man must know death as to his own will."

John Woolman, *The Journal and Major Essays of John Woolman*, p 176.

1. SELF-SACRIFICE

Jesus:

And to love him with all the heart, and with all the understanding, and with all the soul, and with all the strength, and to love his neighbour as himself, is more than all whole burnt offerings and sacrifices. And when Jesus saw that he answered discreetly, he said unto him, "Thou art not far from the kingdom of God." And no man after that durst ask him any question.

Mark 12:33–34 (AV).

But to do good and to communicate forget not: for with such sacrifices God is well pleased.

Hebrews 13:16 (AV).

Tanakh:

True sacrifice to God is a contrite spirit;
God, You will not despise
a contrite and crushed heart.

Tanakh: The Holy Scriptures. Psalms 51:19.

He who sacrifices a thank offering honors Me,
    and to him who improves his way
I will show the salvation of God.

Tanakh: The Holy Scriptures. Psalms 50:23.

EQUALITY TESTIMONY 1

Zarathushtra:

That Holy-Word of Sacrifice went forth
> From God—one with Eternal Law;
God Himself hath in this Word ordained
> The sweets of Mother-Earth to all who serve.

The Divine Songs of Zarathushtra. Ahunavaiti 1.7—Yasna 29.7.

When She appeals for every open doubt,
> Or when, O God, secret ones She solves;
Or when for mere trifling lapse a man
> To long and dire penances submits;—
All this Thou watchest with Thy radiant Eye,
> And close observ'st, as laid down in Thy Law.

The Divine Songs of Zarathushtra. Ahunavaiti 4.13—Yasna 31.13.

Krishna:

If this is beyond your powers,
dedicate yourself to me;
performing all actions for my sake,
you will surely achieve success.

Bhagavad Gita. 12.10.

1. SELF-SACRIFICE

The whole world becomes a slave
to its own activity, Arjuna;
if you want to be truly free,
perform all actions as worship.

Bhagavad Gita. 3.9.

Buddha:

Come, look at this glittering world, like unto a royal chariot; the foolish are immersed in it, but the discerning do not cling to it.

The Dhammapada. 13:171.

One should not therefore hold anything dear. Its loss is grievous. Those who hold nothing dear and hate nothing have no fetters.

The Dhammapada. 16:211.

Muhammad's Revelation:

Say: "Behold, my prayer, and [all] my acts of worship, and my living and my dying are for God [alone], the Sustainer of all the worlds, in whose divinity none has a share: for thus have I been bidden — and I shall [always] be foremost among those who surrender themselves unto Him."

The Qur'an. Al-'An 'am (Cattle) 6:162-163.

EQUALITY TESTIMONY 1

Meher Baba:

No sacrifice is too big to set man free from spiritual bondage and help him to inherit the Truth, which alone shall bring abiding peace to all and which alone will sustain an unassailable sense of universal fellowhood—cemented by the ungrudging love of all, for all, as expressions of the same Reality.

Meher Baba, *Discourses*, 7th edition. P. 343.

The aspirant is always willing to offer everything for the divine Beloved, and no sacrifice is too difficult for him. All his thoughts are turned away from the self and come to be exclusively centered on the divine Beloved.

Meher Baba, *Discourses*, 7th edition. P. 115.

"Wise is the lesson by thy prophet taught;
Woe unto him who judges and forgets
What hidden evil his own heart besets!
Something of this large charity I find
In all the sects that sever humankind;
I would to Allah that their lives agreed
More nearly with the lesson of their creed!"

John Greenleaf Whittier, "Miriam," in *The Complete Poetical Works of John Greenleaf Whittier*, p 341-347.

EQUALITY PRINCIPLE 2

LOVE IS TAKING RESPONSIBILITY

If, instead of seeing faults in others, we look within ourselves, we are loving God.

<u>Quakers:</u>

"...for the truth never grows old, but is the same for ever, & those that Abides in it Lives unto god for ever, & soe Let all things Rest, for I beeleve there is noe ill intentions in any —& soe the Lord god Almighty, Keep us all in Love & unity with god, & with one Another, & then all will be well...".

Margaret Fell, *Undaunted Zeal: The Letters of Margaret Fell*, "To Sarah Fell Meade December 11, 1693," p. 455.

"Not all people receive and obey the Light within. All have the ability to reason, but not all are reasonable. Is it the fault of the grain stored in the granary that it does not grow, or of money hidden in a napkin that it does not earn interest? So, if those who object will tell us whose fault it is that some have wasted their gift, we are prepared to tell them why the unprofitable servant was not rewarded. The blind must not blame the sun for their blindness, nor should sinners accus Grace of being inadequate."

William Penn, *Twenty-First Century Penn*, "Primitive Christianity Revived," 1696, p. 301.

2. LOVE IS TAKING RESPONSIBILITY

"There is, therefore, the greater responsibility that we first examine ourselves and ascertain what there is for us to do in order that we may speedily rid ourselves of the great evil that is clinging to us. Evil? — this mighty sin which so easily besets us. There are those here who have had their hearts touched, who have been led to feel and have entered into sympathy with the bondman, and have known where the evil lies....There are many disposed to examine, to cultivate their minds and hearts in relation to their duties in this respect. May you be faithful, and enter into a consideration as to how far you are partakers in this evil, even in other men's sins. How far, by permission, by apology, or otherwise you are found lending your sanction to a system which degrades and brutalizes three millions of our fellow beings; which denies to them the rights of intelligent education, rights essential to them, and which we acknowledge to be dear to us."

Lucretia Mott, *Lucretia Mott Speaks: The Essential Speeches and Sermons*, "'Sermon to the Medical Students, Cherry Street Meeting, Philadelphia, February 11, 1849,'" p. 52.

Jesus:

"Judge not that ye be not judged. For with what judgment ye judge, ye shall be judged: and with what measure ye mete, it shall be measured to you again. And why beholdest thou the mote that is in thy brother's eye, but considerest not the beam that is in thine own eye?... first cast out the beam out of thine own eye; and then shalt thou see clearly to cast out the mote out of thy brother's eye."

Matthew 7:1–5 (AV).

EQUALITY TESTIMONY 2

Tanakh:

He who seeks love overlooks faults,
But he who harps on a matter alienates his friend.
A rebuke works on an intelligent man
More than one hundred blows on a fool.

Tanakh: The Holy Scriptures. Proverbs 17:9–10.

You shall not take vengeance or bear a grudge against your countrymen. Love your fellow as yourself: I am the Lord.

Tanakh: The Holy Scriptures. Leviticus 19:18.

Zarathushtra:

The strong wise man, guided by Law Divine,
Or by his human heart, kindly receives
All suppliants who come, though they be False;
    He follows Knowledge's Path, he lives for Truth,
      Their erring steps from soul destroying ways
      To Self-reliance wisely shall he guide.

The Divine Songs of Zarathushtra. Ustavaiti 4.5—Yasna 46.5.

Krishna:

Fearlessness, purity of heart,
persistence in the yoga of knowledge,
generosity, self-control,
nonviolence, gentleness, candor,...

2. LOVE IS TAKING RESPONSIBILITY

these are the qualities of men
born with divine traits, Arjuna.

Bhagavad Gita. 16.1, 3.

Buddha:

Not the perversities of others, not what they have done or left undone should a sage take notice of.

The Dhammapada. 4:50.

The fault of others is easily perceived, but that of one's self is difficult to perceive; a man winnows his neighbours' faults like chaff, but hides his own, even as a dishonest gambler hides a losing throw.

The Dhammapada. 18:252.

Muhammad's Revelation:

And never concern thyself with anything of which thou hast no knowledge: verily, [thy] hearing and sight and heart – all of them – will be called to account for it [on Judgment Day]!

The Qur'an. Al-ʾIsrāaʾ (The Night Journey) 17:36.

EQUALITY TESTIMONY 2

Now those people have passed away; unto them shall be accounted what they have earned, and unto you, what you have earned; and you will not be judged on the strength of what they did.

The Qur'an. Al-Baqarah (The Cow) 2:141.

Meher Baba:

...When a person avoids backbiting and thinks more of the good points in others than of their bad points, and when he can practice supreme tolerance and desires good for others even at cost to himself—he is ready to receive the grace of the Master.

Meher Baba, *Discourses*, 7th edition. P. 114.

O, then, if gleams of truth and light
    Flash o'er thy waiting mind,
Unfolding to thy mental sight
    The wants of human-kind;
If, brooding over human grief,
    The earnest wish is known
To soothe and gladden with relief
    An anguish not thine own;

Though heralded with naught of fear,
    Or outward sign or show;
Though only to the inward ear
    It whispers soft and low;
Though dropping, as the manna fell,
    Unseen, yet from above,
Noiseless as dew-fall, heed it well, –
    Thy Father's call of love!

John Greenleaf Whittier, "The Call of the Christian," in *The Complete Poetical Works of John Greenleaf Whittier*, p 92.

EQUALITY PRINCIPLE 3

LOVE IS GRATITUDE

If, instead of worrying over our own misfortunes, we think of ourselves more fortunate than many, many others, we are loving God.

Quakers:

"There are many now rather doubting whether the feelings they have are indeed all that they are to look for — whether it is He that shall come or look we for another. My young friends, you have both seen him, and it is he that talketh with you, and if you receive him in the hour of his coming, in simplicity and lowliness, in the little duties presented to you, perhaps among your young companions, ye shall see greater things than these; ye shall go on until ye can acknowledge that this is indeed He that shall come into the world; and great will be your blessing; great will be your peace; and when that peace which passeth understanding shall be yours, then will the language of praise ascend; and you will be made to rejoice evermore, and, in all things, to give thanks."

Lucretia Mott, *Lucretia Mott Speaks: The Essential Speeches and Sermons*, "Fifteenth Street Meeting, New York City, November 11, 1866," p. 159.

"And in some places our way was more difficult, and I often saw the necessity of keeping down to that root from whence our concern proceeded, and have cause in reverent thankfulness humbly to bow down before the Lord, who was near to me and preserved my mind in calmness under some sharp conflicts and begat a spirit of sympathy and tenderness in me toward some

3. LOVE IS GRATITUDE

who were grievously entangled in the spirit of this world."

John Woolman, *The Journal and Major Essays of John Woolman*, p 96.

Jesus:

Jesus looked up and saw the rich putting their gifts into the offering box, and he saw a poor widow put in two small copper coins. And he said, "Truly, I tell you, this poor widow has put in more than all of them. For they all contributed out of their abundance, but she out of her poverty put in all she had to live on."

Luke 21:1–4 (AV).

Tanakh:

Many say, "O for good days!"
Bestow Your favor on us, O Lord.
You put joy into my heart
      when their grain and wine show increase.
Safe and sound, I lie down and sleep,
      for You alone, O Lord, keep me secure.

Tanakh: The Holy Scriptures. Psalms 4:7–9.

When you have eaten your fill, give thanks to the Lord your God for the good land which He has given you.

Tanakh: The Holy Scriptures. Deuteronomy 8:10.

EQUALITY TESTIMONY 3

Zarathushtra:

One who always thinks of his own safety and profit, how can he love the joy-bringing Mother Earth? The righteous man that follows Knowledge's Law shall dwell in regions radiant with Thy Sun, the abode where wise ones dwell.

Mobed Firouz Azargoshasb, *Translation of Gathas: The Holy Songs Of Zarathushtra*. (2017: https://www.zarathushtra.com). Yasna 50, Verse 2.

How shall one woo joy-bringing Mother Earth,
While thinking thoughts of his own selfish gains?
The Righteous man, that follows Knowledge's Law,
Shall dwell in regions radiant with Thy Sun,
His place shall be in Wisdom's own Abode.

The Divine Songs of Zarathushtra. Spenta-Mainyu 4.2—Yasna 50.2.

Krishna:

[Wise men] do not rejoice in good fortune;
they do not lament at bad fortune;
lucid, with minds unshaken,
they remain within what is real.

Bhagavad Gita. 5.20.

The wise man, cleansed of his sins,
who has cut off all separation,
who delights in the welfare of all beings,

3. LOVE IS GRATITUDE

vanishes into God's bliss.

Bhagavad Gita. 5.25.

Buddha:

Let him not disdain what he has received, let him not envy others; a monk who envies others does not attain (the tranquility of) meditation.

The Dhammapada. 25:365.

Muhammad's Revelation:

Guide us in the straight way – the way of those upon whom Thou hast bestowed Thy blessings, not of those who have been condemned [by Thee], nor of those who go astray.

The Qur'an. Al-Fātihah (The Opening) 1:6–7.

Meher Baba:

One of the greatest obstacles hindering this spiritual preparation of the aspirant is worry. When, with supreme effort, this obstacle of worry is overcome, a way is paved for the cultivation of the divine attributes that constitute the spiritual preparation of the disciple.

Meher Baba, *Discourses*, 7th edition. P. 114.

EQUALITY TESTIMONY 3

Worry is the product of feverish imagination working under the stimulus of desires. It is the living through of sufferings that are mostly of one's own creation. Worry has never done anyone any good; and it is very much worse than mere dissipation of energy, for it substantially curtails the joy and fullness of life.

Meher Baba, *Discourses*, 7th edition. P. 358.

"Shall souls redeemed by me refuse
To share my sorrow in their turn?
Or, sin-forgiven, my gift abuse
      Of peace with selfish unconcern?
Has saintly ease no pitying care?
      Has faith no work, and love no prayer?
While sin remains, and souls in darkness dwell,
Can heaven itself be heaven, and look unmoved on hell?"

John Greenleaf Whittier, "Divine Compassion," in *The Complete Poetical Works of John Greenleaf Whittier*, p 339.

EQUALITY PRINCIPLE 4

HELP AND SERVE OTHERS

With the understanding that God is in everyone, try to help and serve others.

Quakers:

We shall experience a reward, for true it is, that those who go forth, thus ministering to the wants and necessities of their fellow beings, experience a rich return—their souls being as a watered garden, as a spring that faileth not.

Lucretia Mott, *Lucretia Mott Speaks: The Essential Speeches and Sermons*, "Cherry Street Meeting, Philadelphia, March 31, 1850," p. 85.

From an inward purifying, and steadfast abiding under it springs a lively operative desire for the good of others....The outward modes of worship are various; but whenever any are true ministers of Jesus Christ, it is from the operation of his Spirit upon their hearts, first purifying them, and thus giving them a just sense of the conditions of others.

John Woolman, Harvard Classics, *The Journal of John Woolman*, 1779. (New York, NY: P.F. Collier and Son Corporation, 1937), p. 176.

Jesus:

"But when thou makest a feast, call the poor, the maimed, the lame, the blind: And thou shalt be blessed; for they cannot recompense thee: for thou shalt be recompensed at

4. HELP AND SERVE OTHERS

the resurrection of the just."

Luke 14:13-14 (AV).

Tanakh:

Do not withhold good from one who deserves it
When you have the power to do it [for him].

Tanakh: The Holy Scriptures. Proverbs 3:27.

It is to share your bread with the hungry,
And to take the wretched poor into your home;
When you see the naked, to clothe him,
And not to ignore your own kin.
Then shall your light burst through like the dawn
And your healing spring up quickly.

Tankah: The Holy Scriptures. Isaiah 58:7-8.

Zarathushtra:

Such are, indeed, the Saviours of the Earth,
They follow Duty's call, the call of Love :
God, they listen unto Love;
    They do what Knowledge bids, and Thy Commands;
    Surely they are the Vanquishers of Hate.

The Divine Songs of Zarathushtra. Spenta-Mainyu 2.12—Yasna 48.12.

EQUALITY TESTIMONY 4

Krishna:

The same to both friend and foe,
the same in disgrace or honor,
suffering or joy, untroubled,
indifferent to praise or blame,...
that man is the one I love best.

Bhagavad Gita. 12.18, 19.

Knowledge that sees in all things
a single, imperishable being,
undivided among the divided—
this kind of knowledge is *sattvic*.[*]

Bhagavad Gita. 18.20.

Buddha:

In like manner his good works receive him who has done good, and has gone from this world to the other; — as kinsmen receive one who is dear to them on his return.

The Dhammapada. 16:220.

The disciples of Gotama are always wide awake and watchful, and their mind day and night ever delights in compassion.

The Dhammapada. 21:300.

---

[*] *Sattva* is characterized as "pure"; in Hinduism it represents the principle of pure thought.

4. HELP AND SERVE OTHERS

Muhammad's Revelation:

[The truly virtuous are] they...who give food – however great be their own want of it – unto the needy, and the orphan, and the captive, [saying, in their hearts,] "We feed you for the sake of God alone: we desire no recompense from you, nor thanks"

The Qur'an. Al-'Insan (Man) 76:7-9.

Meher Baba:

And in being useful to a fellow aspirant in doing the Master's work, the aspirant is rendering a service to him as much as to the Master.
Meher Baba, Discourses, 7th edition. P. 364
The life of the Man-God is a life of service; it is a perpetual offering to other forms of his own Self.

Meher Baba, *Discourses*, 7th edition. P. 93.

EQUALITY TESTIMONY 4

I ask not now for gold to gild
    With mocking shine a weary frame;
The yearning of the mind is stilled, –
    I ask not now for Fame.

A rose-cloud, dimly seen above,
    Melting in heaven's blue depths away, –
O, sweet, fond dream of human Love!
    For thee I may not pray.

But, bowed in lowliness of mind,
    I make my humble wishes known, –
I only ask a will resigned,
    O Father, to thine own!

To-day, beneath thy chastening eye
    I crave alone for peace and rest,
Submissive in thy hand to lie,
    And feel that it is best.

John Greenleaf Whittier, "The Wish of To-Day," in *The Complete Poetical Works of John Greenleaf Whittier*, p 150.

EQUALITY PRINCIPLE 5

HUMILITY

If you have the humility of earth, which can be molded into any shape, then you will know Me.

Quakers:

"...and it is the Low, and the Meek, and Humble that the Lord God teacheth, and it is the broken and contrite Spirit, that God will not despise [Ps. 51:17]. And he, who is the High and Lofty one, that Inhabiteth Eternity, dwelleth in the Hearts of the Humble."

Margaret Fell, *Undaunted Zeal: The Letters of Margaret Fell*, "An Epistle to Friends 1655," p. 170.

Deep humility is a strong bulwark, and as we enter into it we find safety and true exaltation. The foolishness of God is wiser than man, and the weakness of God is stronger than man. Being unclothed of our own wisdom, and knowing the abasement of the creature, we find that power to arise which gives health and vigor to us.

John Woolman, *The Journal of John Woolman (HC)*, 1756. P. 199.

5. HUMILITY

Jesus:

"And I say unto you, Make to yourselves friends of the mammon of unrighteousness; that, when ye fail, they may receive you into everlasting habitations. He that is faithful in that which is least is faithful also in much: and he that is unjust in the least is unjust also in much. If therefore ye have not been faithful in the unrighteous mammon, who will commit to your trust the true riches? And if ye have not been faithful in that which is another man's, who shall give you that which is your own? No servant can serve two masters: for either he will hate the one, and love the other; or else he will hold to the one, and despise the other. Ye cannot serve God and mammon."

Luke 16:9–13 (AV).

Humble yourselves therefore under the mighty hand of God, that he may exalt you in due time: Casting all your care upon him; for he careth for you.

1 Peter 5:6–7 (AV).

Tanakh:

"Your hands shaped and fashioned me,
Then destroyed every part of me.
Consider that You fashioned me like clay;
Will you then turn me back into dust?"

Tanakh: The Holy Scriptures. Job 10:8–9.

EQUALITY TESTIMONY 5

When arrogance appears, disgrace follows,
But wisdom is with those who are unassuming.

Tanakh: The Holy Scriptures. Proverbs 11:2.

Zarathushtra:

All Holy Lives are put into Thy Hands,
    All that have been, and all that are today,
    And all, O God, that shall ever be;
Out of Thy Grace permit us these to share;
    Through Love of Man, through Service and through Truth,
    Raise Thou our Souls into Thy Realms of Light.

The Divine Songs of Zarathushtra. Ahunavaiti 6.10—Yasna 33.10.

Krishna:

Humility, patience, sincerity,
nonviolence, uprightness, purity,
devotion to one's spiritual teacher,
constancy, self-control,...

all this is called true knowledge;
what differs from it is called ignorance.

Bhagavad Gita. 13.7, 11.

...dignity, kindness, courage,
a benevolent, loving heart—
these are the qualities of men
born with divine traits, Arjuna.

Bhagavad Gita. 16.3.

Buddha:

Such a man who does his duty is tolerant like the earth, like a stone set in a threshold; he is like a lake without mud; no new births are in store for him.

The Dhammapada. 7:95.

Irrigators guide the water (wherever they like); fletchers bend the arrow; carpenters bend a log of wood; good people fashion themselves.

The Dhammapada. 10:145.

Muhammad's Revelation:

"And turn not thy cheek away from people in [false] pride, and walk not haughtily on earth: for, behold, God does not love anyone who, out of self-conceit, acts in a boastful manner. Hence, be modest in thy bearing, and lower thy voice: for, behold, the ugliest of all voices is the [loud] voice of asses...".

The Qur'an. Luqman 31:18-19.

5. HUMILITY

Verily, God does not love any of those who, full of self-conceit, act in a boastful manner....

The Qur'an. An-Nisaa (Women) 4:36.

Meher Baba:

Even a small gift, given with humility and utterly unselfish love, is endowed with much greater spiritual value.

Meher Baba, *Discourses*, 7th edition. P. 119.

In the world of spirituality, humility counts at least as much as utility.

Meher Baba, *Discourses*, 7th edition. P. 364.

O brother man! fold to thy heart thy brother;
    Where pity dwells, the peace of God is there;
To worship rightly is to love each other,
    Each smile a hymn, each kindly deed a prayer.

Follow with reverent steps the great example
    Of Him whose holy work was "doing good";
So shall the wide earth seem our Father's temple,
    Each loving life a psalm of gratitude.

Then shall all shackles fall; the stormy clangor
    Of wild war music o'er the earth shall cease;
Love shall tread out the baleful fire of anger,
    And in its ashes plant the tree of peace!

John Greenleaf Whittier, "Worship," in *The Complete Poetical Works of John Greenleaf Whittier*, p 123-124.

EQUALITY PRINCIPLE 6

SELFLESS SERVICE

If you have the quality of selfless service unaffected by results similar to that of the sun, which serves the world by shining on all creation—on the grass in the field, on the birds in the air, on the beasts in the forest, on all of mankind with its sinners and saints, its rich and poor—unmindful of the attitude toward it, then you will win Me.

Quakers:

"O dear hearts put your hands in this worke, & be not slake [slack], but up & be doing in the name & power of Jesus and in the fear of the Lord, offer freely to his service, that in the freeness & willingnesse of your spirits, the brethren may be refreshed, in & by your freness in your spirets unto the Lord, who beare the heat of the day....the worke & service of the Lord requires of you in the freeness of your spirits, to gather, collect, & contribute in your several meetings for providing, & maintaining of your brethren what [?] nescessaries, whom the Lord hath called out of Late...for every man as he purposeth in his heart, so let him give, not grudgingly nor of necessity for the Lord loves a chearfull giver....".

Margaret Fell, *Undaunted Zeal: The Letters of Margaret Fell*, "To Friends and Brethren 1656," p. 215.

6. SELFLESS SERVICE

In this case I had fresh confirmation that acting contrary to present outward interest, from a motive of Divine love, and in regard to truth and righteousness, and thereby incurring the resentments of people, opens the way to a treasure better than silver, and to a friendship exceeding the friendship of men.

John Woolman, *The Journal of John Woolman (HC)*, 1753, p. 189.

Jesus:

My little children, let us not love in word, neither in tongue; but in deed and in truth. And hereby we know that we are of the truth, and shall assure our hearts before him.

1 John 3:18–19 (AV).

Tanakh:

If, however, there is a needy person among you, one of your kinsmen in any of your settlements in the land that the Lord your God is giving you, do not harden your heart and shut your hand against your needy kinsman. Rather, you must open your hand and lend him sufficient for whatever he needs.... For there will never cease to be needy ones in your land, which is why I command you: open your hand to the poor and needy kinsman in your land.

Tanakh: The Holy Scriptures. Deuteronomy 15:7-8, 11.

EQUALITY TESTIMONY 6

A generous person enjoys prosperity;
He who satisfies others shall himself be sated.

Tanakh: The Holy Scriptures. Proverbs 11:25.

Zarathushtra:

The strong wise man, guided by Law Divine,
Or by his human heart, kindly receives
All suppliants who come, though they be False.

The Divine Songs of Zarathushtra. Ustavaiti 4.5—Yasna 46.5.

Krishna:

With no desire for success,
no anxiety about failure,
indifferent to results, he burns up
his actions in the fire of wisdom.

Bhagavad Gita. 4.19.

He who performs his duty
with no concern for results
is the true man of yoga—not
he who refrains from action.

Bhagavad Gita. 6.1.

6. SELFLESS SERVICE

Buddha:

He whose misdeeds are covered by good deeds, brightens up this world, like the moon when freed from clouds.

The Dhammapada. 13:173.

The disciples of Gotama are always wide awake and watchful, and their mind day and night ever delights in compassion.

The Dhammapada. 21:300.

Muhammad's Revelation:

The parable of those who spend their possessions for the sake of God is that of a grain out of which grows seven ears, in every ear a hundred grains: for God grants manifold increase unto whom He wills; and God is infinite, all-knowing. They who spend their possessions for the sake of God and do not thereafter mar their spending by stressing their own benevolence and hurting [the feelings of the needy] shall have their reward with their Sustainer, and no fear need they have, and neither shall they grieve. A kind word and the veiling of another's want is better than a charitable deed followed by hurt.

The Qur'an. Al-Baqarah (The Cow) 2:261–263.

EQUALITY TESTIMONY 6

Meher Baba:

Selfless service is accomplished when there is not the slightest thought of reward or result, and when there is complete disregard of one's own comfort or convenience or the possibility of being misunderstood.

Meher Baba, *Discourses*, 7th edition. P. 53.

The real justification for a life of selfless service is to be found in this intrinsic worth of such a life and not in any ulterior result or consequence.

Meher Baba, *Discourses*, 7th edition. P. 263.

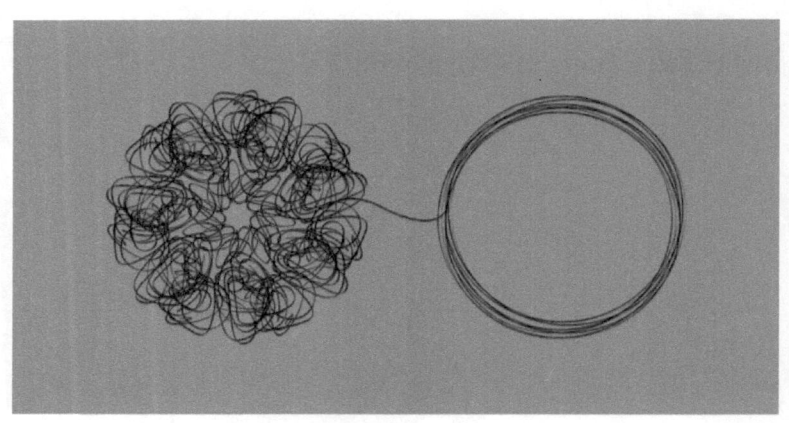

SECTION THREE

SIMPLICITY

Thou judgest us; Thy purity
Doth all our lusts condemn;
The love that draws us nearer Thee
Is hot with wrath to them.

Our thoughts lie open to Thy sight;
And, naked to Thy glance,
Our secret sins are in the light
Of Thy pure countenance.

John Greenleaf Whittier, "Our Master," in *The Complete Poetical Works of John Greenleaf Whittier*, p 319-321.

SIMPLICITY PRINCIPLE 1

RENUNCIATION OF ALL SELFISH THOUGHTS AND DESIRES

The only Real Renunciation is that which abandons, even in the midst of worldly duties, all selfish thoughts and desires.

Quakers:

"I long for you my friends, that you may be so true to your best feelings as to be preserved from the temptations with which you are surrounded, that your hearts may be preserved in unsullied purity. And in so far as any of you have swerved from the right, and have gone down to the chambers of dissipation, or been found in any indulgence from which your better nature would revolt, oh, be persuaded to make a stand in your course, to return, repent, and live. The God with whom we have to do, our tender Father 'who is plenteous in redemption, and abundant in mercy,' requireth only that those who have departed from the right shall return, shall give up their practices and walk uprightly."

Lucretia Mott, *Lucretia Mott Speaks: The Essential Speeches and Sermons*, "'Sermon to the Medical Students, Cherry Street Meeting, Philadelphia, February 11, 1849,'" p. 53.

"All Christians ought to be circumcised by the Spirit, which puts off the body of the sins of the flesh, that they may come to eat of the heavenly sacrifice, Christ Jesus, that true spiritual food, which none can rightly feed upon but that they are cir

1. RENUNCIATION

cumcised by the spirit."

George Fox, 1649, *The Journal of George Fox*, "Fox and Children's Training," 1649. (London, J.M. Dent & Sons, 1924), p. 34.

"Divine love imposeth no rigorous or unreasonable commands, but graciously points out the spirit of brotherhood and way to happiness, in the attaining to which it is necessary that we go forth out of all that is selfish."

John Woolman, *The Journal and Major Essays of John Woolman*, "A Plea For The Poor," p 242.

"To labour for an establishment in divine love where the mind is disentangled from the power of darkness is the great business of man's life. Collecting of riches, covering the body with fine-wrought, costly apparel, and having magnificent furniture operates against universal love and tends to feed self, that to desire these things belongs not to the children of the Light."

John Woolman, *The Journal and Major Essays of John Woolman*, "A Plea For The Poor," p 250.

Jesus:

There hath no temptation taken you but such as is common to man: but God is faithful, who will not suffer you to be tempted above that ye are able; but will with the temptation also make a way to escape, that ye may be able to bear it.

1 Corinthians 10:13 (AV).

SIMPLICITY TESTIMONY 1

Let nothing be done through strife or vainglory; but in lowliness of mind let each esteem other better than themselves. Look not every man on his own things, but every man also on the things of others.

Philippians 2: 3-4 (KJV).

Tanakh:

Now say to the House of Israel: Thus said the Lord God: Repent, and turn back from your fetishes and turn your minds away from all your abominations.

Tanakh: The Holy Scriptures. Ezekiel 14:6.

Teach me, O Lord, the way of Your laws;
   I will observe them to the utmost.
Give me understanding, that I may observe Your teaching
   and keep it wholeheartedly.
Lead me in the path of Your commandments,
   for that is my concern.
Turn my heart to Your decrees
   and not to love of gain.
Avert my eyes from seeing falsehood;
   by Your ways preserve me.

Tanakh: The Holy Scriptures. Psalms 119:33-37.

1. RENUNCIATION

Zarathushtra:

Thy Holy Spirit frustrates Evil Ones,
But not, O God, any Truthful Man;
    A man of small possessions here below
    Inclines unto the Truth, but he who hath
    Great riches is unfortunate, O Lord.

The Divine Songs of Zarathushtra. Spenta-Mainyu 1.4—Yasna 47.4.

God, Thou hast laid down that man shall choose
The Path of Truth and thus frustrate Untruth;
    The Path of Truth is but the Path of Love,
    Therefore, should man commune with Love,
    And should renounce all contact with Untruth.

The Divine Songs of Zarathushtra. Spenta-Mainyu 3.3—Yas. 49.3.

Krishna:

When a man gives up all desires
that emerge from the mind, and rests
contented in the Self by the Self,
he is called a man of firm wisdom.

Bhagavad Gita. 2.55.

The true renunciate neither
desires things nor avoids them;
indifferent to pleasure and pain,

he is easily freed from all bondage.

Bhagavad Gita. 5.3.

Buddha:

What now is the Noble Truth of the Extinction of Suffering? It is the complete fading away and extinction of this craving, its forsaking and giving up, the liberation and detachment from it. But where may this craving vanish, where may it be extinguished? Wherever in the world there are delightful and pleasurable things, there this craving may vanish, there it may be extinguished.

A Buddhist Bible. P. 31.

Muhammad's Revelation:

Alluring unto man is the enjoyment of worldly desires through women, and children, and heaped-up treasures of gold and silver, and horses of high mark, and cattle, and lands. All this may be enjoyed in the life of this world – But the most beauteous of all goals is with God.... For the God-conscious there are, with their Sustainer, gardens through which running waters flow, therein to abide, and spouses pure, and God's goodly acceptance.

The Qur'an. ʾĀl-ʿImrān (The House of ʿImrān) 3:14–15.

1. RENUNCIATION

And thus have We willed you to be a community of the middle way, so that [with your lives] you might bear witness to the truth before all mankind.

The Qur'an. Al-Baqarah (The Cow) 2:143.

Meher Baba:

Spirituality does not require the external renunciation of worldly activities or the avoiding of duties and responsibilities. It only requires that, while performing the worldly activities or discharging the responsibilities arising from the specific place and position of the individual, the inner spirit should remain free from the burden of desires.

Meher Baba, *Discourses*, 7th edition. P. 15.

SIMPLICITY TESTIMONY 1

THE Quaker of the olden time!
How calm and firm and true,
Unspotted by its wrong and crime,
He walked the dark earth through.
The lust of power, the love of gain,
The thousand lures of sin
Around him, had no power to stain
The purity within.

John Greenleaf Whittier, "The Quaker of Olden Time," in *The Complete Poetical Works of John Greenleaf Whittier*, p 98.

SIMPLICITY PRINCIPLE 2

REAL CONTROL IS DISCIPLINE OF THE SENSES

The only Real Control is the discipline of the senses from indulgence in low desires, which alone ensures absolute purity of character.

Quakers:

"And so dear Friends above all mind your Spiritual Freedom, and your Spiritual Reward, which will be sure to be received, according to every one's Deeds done in the Body; he that doth good Deeds in the Body, will receive good; He that doth Evil Deeds in the Body, he shall receive his Reward accordingly."

Margaret Fell, *Undaunted Zeal: The Letters of Margaret Fell*, "An Epistle to Friends June 7, 1664," p. 377.

"As I have sometimes been much spent in the heat and taken spirits to revive me, I have found by experience that in such circumstance the mind is not so calm nor so fitly disposed for divine meditation as when all such extremes are avoided, and have felt an increasing care to attend to that Holy Spirit which sets right bounds to our desires and leads those who faithfully follow it to apply all the gifts of divine providence to the purposes for which they were intended."

John Woolman, *The Journal and Major Essays of John Woolman*, p 55.

2. REAL CONTROL IS DISCIPLINE OF THE SENSES

Jesus:

For he that soweth to his flesh shall of the flesh reap corruption; but he that soweth to the Spirit shall of the Spirit reap life everlasting.

Galatians 6:8 (AV).

This I say then, Walk in the Spirit, and ye shall not fulfill the lust of the flesh.

Galatians 5:16 (AV).

Tanakh:

O Lord, remember in David's favor
      his extreme self-denial,
      how he swore to the Lord,
      vowed to the Mighty One of Jacob,
      "I will not enter my house,
      nor will I mount my bed,
      I will not give sleep to my eyes,
      or slumber to my eyelids
      until I find a place for the Lord,
      an abode for the Mighty One of Jacob."

Tanakh: The Holy Scriptures. Psalms 132:1–5.

Speak to the Israelite people and instruct them to make for themselves fringes on the corners of their garments throughout the ages; let them attach a cord of blue to the frings at each corner. That shall be your fringe; look at it and recall all the commandments of the Lord and observe them, so that you do not follow your heart and eyes in your lustful urge.

Tanakh: The Holy Scriptures. Numbers 14:38-39.

Zarathushtra:

But, God, he who through the urge of heart,
Through sacrifice of Self, doth link himself,
And his own Inner Self with Love,
> Finds Wisdom, and Knowledge's Wisdom, too;
> > Sheltered by Righteousness, he shall dwell with Them.

The Divine Songs of Zarathushtra. Spenta-Mainyu 3.5—Yasna 49.5.

Krishna:

But the man who is self-controlled,
who meets the objects of the senses
with neither craving nor aversion,
will attain serenity at last.

In serenity, all his sorrows
disappear at once, forever;
when his heart has become serene,

2. REAL CONTROL IS DISCIPLINE OF THE SENSES

his understanding is steadfast.

Bhagavad Gita. 2.64–65.

The superior man is he
whose mind can control his senses;
with no attachment to results,
he engages in the yoga of action.

Bhagavad Gita. 3.6–7.

Buddha:

'All existing things are unreal.' He who knows and perceives this is no longer [in] the thrall of grief.

The Dhammapada. 20:279.

Muhammad's Revelation:

But nay — they who are bent on evildoing follow but their own desires, without having any knowledge [of the truth]. And who could guide those whom God has [thus] let go astray, and who [thereupon] have none to succour them? And so, set thy face steadfastly towards the [one ever-true] faith, turning away from all that is false, in accordance with the natural disposition which God has instilled into man: [for,] not to allow any change to corrupt what God has thus created — this is the [purpose of the one] ever-true faith; but most people know it not. [Turn, then, away from all that is false,] turning unto Him [alone]; and remain conscious of Him, and be constant in prayer, and be not

SIMPLICITY TESTIMONY 2

among those who ascribe divinity to aught beside Him.

The Qur'an. Ar-Rum (The Byzantines) 30:29-31.

Meher Baba:

Control of the habitual tendencies of the mind is much more difficult than control of physical actions. The fleeting and evasive thoughts and desires of the mind can be curbed only with great patience and persistent practice. But the restraint of mental processes and reactions is necessary to check the formation of new sanskaras˙ and to wear out or unwind the old sanskaras of which they are expressions. Though control might be difficult at the beginning, through sincere effort it gradually becomes natural and easy to achieve.

Meher Baba, *Discourses*, 7th edition. P. 49.

The mind must turn away from all temptations, and complete control must be established over the senses. Thus control and dispassion are both necessary to attain one-pointedness in the search for true understanding.

Meher Baba, *Discourses*, 7th edition. P. 358.

˙

˙*Impressions; traces or imprints of former experiences left as residue on consciousness that determines one's desires and actions.*

Yet where our duty's task is wrought
In unison with God's great thought,
The near and future blend in one,
And whatsoe'er is willed, is done!

And ours the grateful service whence
Comes, day by day, the recompense;
The hope, the trust, the purpose stayed,
The fountain and the noonday shade.

John Greenleaf Whittier, "Seed-Time and Harvest," in *The Complete Poetical Works of John Greenleaf Whittier*, p 151.

SIMPLICITY PRINCIPLE 3

ATTEND TO YOUR DUTIES BUT DO NOT BE ATTACHED TO RESULTS

Attend faithfully to your worldly duties, but keep always at the back of your mind that all this is God's.

<u>Quakers:</u>

"Let not the mere pleasures of life, allowable as these may be with the proper limitation, allow not these pleasures so to take this place and to fill the heart that there shall be no room for this Beloved of the souls who stands at the heart waiting for entrance until, to use the figurative expression, His 'head is filled with dew, and His locks with the drops of the night.'"

Lucretia Mott, *Lucretia Mott Speaks: The Essential Speeches and Sermons*, "Race Street Meeting, Philadelphia, March 14, 1869," p. 187.

"But the worship which is required of us, is the active use of all our God-given powers, all our faculties, our intellectual as well as our nobler spiritual gifts. All these consecrated to God, to truth, to righteousness, to humanity, and acts in accordance with such consecration, constitute the worship which is needed, and very different from mere Sunday worship paid in oral prayer, in sacred song, or in silent bowing of the head. We are too apt to confound these means to an end, legitimate, acceptable, noble as they are, with the end itself. We are too apt to mistake Sabbath-observances and Sunday worship for that which the Father is seeking from us all — for the obedience which is

3. ATTEND TO YOUR DUTIES BUT DO NOT BE ATTACHED

called for."

Lucretia Mott, *Lucretia Mott Speaks: The Essential Speeches and Sermons*, "Fifteenth Street Meeting, New York City, November 11, 1866," p. 154.

"There is employ necessary in social life, and this mortal infection incites me to think whether these social acts of mine are real duties. If I go on a visit to the widows and fatherless, do I go purely on a principle of charity, free from every selfish view? If I go to a religious meeting it puts me athinking whether I go in sincerity and in a clear sense of duty, or whether it is not partly in conformity to custom, or partly from a sensible delight which my animal spirits feel in the company of other people, and whether to support my reputation as a religious man has not share in it."

John Woolman, *The Journal and Major Essays of John Woolman*, p. 103.

Jesus:

"But lay up for yourselves treasures in heaven, where neither moth nor rust doth corrupt, and where thieves do not break through nor steal: For where your treasure is, there will your heart be also."

Matthew 6:20–21 (AV).

"Let your light so shine before men, that they may see your good works, and glorify your Father which is in heaven."

Matthew 5:16 (AV).

SIMPLICITY TESTIMONY 3

Tanakh:

What real value is there for a man
In all the gains he makes beneath the sun?

One generation goes, another comes,
But the earth remains the same forever.
The sun rises, and the sun sets—
And glides back to where it rises....
All such things are wearisome:
No man can ever state them;
The eye never has enough of seeing,
Nor the ear enough of hearing.
Only that shall happen
Which has happened,
Only that occur
Which has occurred;
There is nothing new
Beneath the sun!

Tanakh: The Holy Scriptures. Ecclesiastes 1:3–5, 8–9.

Who am I and who are my people, that we should have the means to make such a freewill offering; but all is from You, and it is Your gift that we have given to You. For we are sojourners with You, mere transients like our fathers; our days on earth are like a shadow, with nothing in prospect.

Tanakh: The Holy Scriptures. I Chronicles 29:14-15.

3. ATTEND TO YOUR DUTIES BUT DO NOT BE ATTACHED

Zarathushtra:

The path, O God, which Thou hast shown me is the path of Love, the path based on the teachings of Saoshyants, the saviors. The teaching which recommends that the work performed with the view of performing one's duty honestly shall bring forth happiness. The teaching which leads mankind to real knowledge and wisdom, and reaching Thee O God, is its rewards.

Translation of Gathas: The Holy Songs of Zarathushtra. Yasna 34, Verse 13.

The Path, O God, of Love,
That One Path hast Thou pointed out to me, —
The ancient Teaching of all Saviours,—
That good deeds done for their own sake lead far:—
This Teaching leads mankind to Wisdom true,
That single Prize of Life—Thyself the Goal.

The Divine Songs of Zarathushtra. Ahunavaiti 7.13—Yasna 34.13.

Krishna:

The whole world becomes a slave
to its own activity, Arjuna;
if you want to be truly free,
perform all actions as worship.

Bhagavad Gita. 3.9.

When a man sees clearly that there is
no doer besides the gunas
and knows what exists beyond them,
he can enter my state of being.

Bhagavad Gita. 14.19.

Buddha:

Such a man who does his duty is tolerant like the earth, like a stone set in a threshold; he is like a lake without mud; no new births are in store for him.

The Dhammapada. 7:95.

Muhammad's Revelation:

But woe unto those who deny the truth: for suffering severe awaits those who choose the life of this world as the sole object of their love, preferring it to [all thought of] the life to come, and who turn others away from the path of God and try to make it appear crooked. Such as these have indeed gone far astray!

The Qur'an. 'Ibrāhīm (Abraham) 14:2–3.

...people whom neither [worldly] commerce nor striving after gain can divert from the remembrance of God.

The Qur'an. An-Nūr (The Light) 24:37.

3. ATTEND TO YOUR DUTIES BUT DO NOT BE ATTACHED

Meher Baba:

Spirituality does not require the external renunciation of worldly activities or the avoiding of duties and responsibilities. It only requires that, while performing the worldly activities or discharging the responsibilities arising from the specific place and position of the individual, the inner spirit should remain free from the burden of desires.

Meher Baba, *Discourses*, 7th edition. P. 15.

SIMPLICITY TESTIMONY 3

Yet, in the maddening maze of things,
    And tossed by storm and flood,
To one fixed stake my spirit clings;
    I know that God is good!

Not mine to look where cherubim
    And seraphs may not see,
But nothing can be good in Him
    Which evil is in me.

The wrong that pains my soul below
    I dare not throne above:
I know not of His hate, – I know
    His goodness and His love.

I dimly guess from blessings known
    Of greater out of sight,
And, with the chastened Psalmist, own
    His judgments too are right.

John Greenleaf Whittier, "The Eternal Goodness," in *The Complete Poetical Works of John Greenleaf Whittier*, p 318-319.

SIMPLICITY PRINCIPLE 4

ACCEPT WHAT COMES TO YOU WITHOUT RESENTMENT

Be resigned to every situation and think honestly and sincerely: "God has placed me in this situation."

Quakers:

"— I would have thee to Remember my deare Love, unto the Lady, and its best for her, to settle, & fix, and fasten her minde upon the Lord, which will bee her onely repose, & comfort, & never matter nore minde outward things, but lett them hang of themselves, & come & goe, as the divine providence orders, for greatest concerne is peace with God, and that shee bee faithfull to his Light & spiritt, that God hath placed in her heart, & obeydient to the measure of grace, that will bring her salvation...".

Margaret Fell, *Undaunted Zeal: The Letters of Margaret Fell*, "To Katherine Evans August 3, 1678," p. 427.

"And now, dear Friends, with respect to the commotions and stirrings of the powers of the earth at this time near us, we are desirous that none of us may be moved thereat, but repose ourselves in the munition of that rock which all these shakings shall not move....For as the truth is but one, and many are made partakers of its spirit, so the world is but one."

John Woolman, *The Journal of John Woolman (HC)*, 1775, p. 191.

4. ACCEPT WHAT COMES WITHOUT RESENTMENT

"I rejoice that we are so constituted by our nature that we can, and do accommodate ourselves to the circumstances in which we are placed; and while we may be far from viewing those who are living in self-indulgence, luxury and excess as peculiarly blest of God, or even as desirable to emulate, at the same time we must admit that God, in his wisdom, in his unbounded and illimitable benevolence, has abundantly crowned the earth with blessings, and given unto man of his abundance, richly to enjoy; and that it is desirable that all classes of Society partake of these rich blessings."

Lucretia Mott, *Lucretia Mott Speaks: The Essential Speeches and Sermons*, "Cherry Street Meeting, Philadelphia, March 31, 1850," p. 83.

Jesus:

Go to now, ye that say, To day or to morrow we will go into such a city, and continue there a year, and buy and sell, and get gain: Whereas ye know not what shall be on the morrow. For what is your life? It is even a vapour, that appeareth for a little time, and then vanisheth away. For that ye ought to say, If the Lord will, we shall live, and do this, or that.

James 4:13-15 (KJV).

Tanakh:

What value, then, can the man of affairs get from what he earns? I have observed the business that God gave man to be concerned with: He brings everything to pass precisely at its time; He also puts eternity in their mind, but without man ever guessing, from first to last, all the things that God brings to pass. Thus I realized that the only worthwhile thing there is for them is to enjoy themselves and do what is good in their lifetime; also, that whenever a man does eat and drink and get enjoyment out of all his wealth, it is a gift of God.

Tanakh: The Holy Scriptures. Ecclesiastes 3:9–13.

And should you ask, "What are we to eat in the seventh year, if we may neither sow nor gather in our crops?" I will ordain My blessing for you in the sixth year, so that it shall yield a crop sufficient for three years. When you sow in the eighth year, you will still be eating old grain of that crop; you will be eating the old until the ninth year, until its crops come in. But the land must not be sold beyond reclaim, for the land is Mine; you are but strangers resident with Me.

Tanakh: The Holy Scriptures. Leviticus 25: 20-23.

Zarathushtra:

Of all these sinners none doth understand
    What true and lasting progress might imply,
This can be learnt from Life on earth alone,—
    The "test of molten brass" proclaimed by Thee;
The final end of sinners, God,
    Were best, O God, judged by Thee alone.

The Divine Songs of Zarathushtra. Ahunavaiti 5.7—Yasna 32.7.

Krishna:

When a man has become unattached
to sense-objects or to actions,

4. ACCEPT WHAT COMES WITHOUT RESENTMENT

renouncing his own selfish will,
then he is mature in yoga.

Bhagavad Gita. 6.4.

...detachment, absence of clinging
to son, wife, family, and home,
an unshakeable equanimity
in good fortune or in bad,...
all this is called true knowledge;
what differs from it is called ignorance.

Bhagavad Gita. 13.9, 11.

Buddha:

Patience, long-suffering, is the highest form of penance, Nirvana that highest of all things, say the Awakened.

The Dhammapada. 14:184.

Victory breeds hatred, for the conquered is unhappy. He who has given up both victory and defeat, he, the contented, is happy.

The Dhammapada. 15:201.

Muhammad's Revelation:

"God does not burden any human being with more than he is well able to bear: in his favour shall be whatever good he does,

4. ACCEPT WHAT COMES WITHOUT RESENTMENT

and against him whatever evil he does."

The Qur'an. Al-Baqarah (The Cow) 2:286.

Your Sustainer is fully aware of what you are [and what you deserve]: if He so wills, He will bestow [His] grace upon you; and if He so wills, He will chastise you.

The Qur'an. Al-Israa (The Night Journey) 17:54.

Yet, when a good thing happens to them, some [people] say, "This is from God," whereas when evil befalls them, they say, "This is from thee [O fellow-man]! Say: "All is from God."

The Qur'an. An-Nisaa (Women) 4:78.

Meher Baba:

The self-surrender amounts to an open admission that the aspirant now has given up all hope of tackling the problems of the ego by himself and that he relies solely upon the Master.

Meher Baba, *Discourses*, 7th edition. P. 171.

The shifting of interest from unimportant things to important values is facilitated by allegiance and self-surrender to the Master, who becomes the new nucleus for integration.

Meher Baba, *Discourses*, 7th edition. P. 177.

To Him, from wanderings long and wild,
I come, an over-wearied child,
In cool and shade his peace to find,
Like dew-fall settling on my mind.
Assured that all I know is best,
And humbly trusting for the rest,
I turn from Fancy's cloud-built scheme,
Dark creed, and mournful eastern dream
Of power, impersonal and cold,
Controlling all, itself controlled,
Maker and slave of iron laws,
Alike the subject and the cause;
From vain philosophies, that try
The sevenfold gates of mystery,
And, baffled ever, babble still,
Word-prodigal of fate and will;
From Nature, and her mockery, Art,
And book and speech of men apart,
To the still witness in my heart;
With reverence waiting to behold
His Avatar of love untold,
The Eternal Beauty new and old!

John Greenleaf Whittier, "Questions of Life," in *The Complete Poetical Works of John Greenleaf Whittier*, p 157-159.

SIMPLICITY PRINCIPLE 5

INTEREST IN SENSUAL INDULGENCE NATURALLY FALLS AWAY

When your love for Me drives away your lust for the things of the senses, then you will realize Me.

Quakers:

"We have a natural and a spiritual nature — that which partakes of the animal and that which partakes of the divine nature, and as we receive more of the Divinity dwelling upon the spiritual part we come to have our first nature brought out, and our feelings exalted with the operation of the love of God upon the soul."

Lucretia Mott, *Lucretia Mott Speaks: The Essential Speeches and Sermons*, "Unitarian Church, Washington D.C., January 15, 1843," p. 19.

"And being clearly convinced in my judgment that to place my whole trust in God was best for me, I felt renewed engagements that in all things I might act on an inward principle of virtue and pursue worldly business no further than as Truth opened my way therein."

John Woolman, *The Journal and Major Essays of John Woolman*, 1720-1742, p.32.

5. INTEREST IN SENSUAL INDULGENCE FALLS AWAY

<u>Jesus:</u>

Blessed is the man that endureth temptation: for when he is tried, he shall receive the crown of life, which the Lord hath promised to them that love him. Let no man say when he is tempted, I am tempted of God: for God cannot be tempted with evil, neither tempteth he any man: But every man is tempted, when he is drawn away of his own lust, and enticed.

James 1:12–14 (AV).

For to be carnally minded is death; but to be spiritually minded is life and
peace.

Romans 8:6 (AV).

<u>Tanakh:</u>

"Come, let us reach an understanding,
—says the Lord.
Be your sins like crimson,
They can turn snow-white;
Be they red as dyed wool,
They can become like fleece."
If, then, you agree and give heed,
You will eat the good things of the earth.

Tanakh: The Holy Scriptures. Isaiah 1:18–19.

No longer shall you need the sun
For light by day,
Nor the shining of the moon
For radiance [by night];

For the Lord shall be your light everlasting,
Your God shall be your glory.
Your sun shall set no more,
Your moon no more withdraw;
For the Lord shall be a light to you forever.

Tanakh: The Holy Scriptures. Isaiah 60:19-20.

Zarathushtra:

The false prevents the Righteous everywhere
From helping man along the upward Path;
He worketh not as friend, is dangerous;
Invite him not as helper in your work;
      They who oppose him, God, heart and soul,
      They are true Leaders, they obey Thy Will.

The Divine Songs of Zarathushtra. Ustavaiti 4.4—Yasna 46.4.

Krishna:

When a man gives up all desires
that emerge from the mind, and rests
contented in the Self by the Self,
he is called a man of firm wisdom.

Bhagavad Gita. 2.55.

Restraining the senses, disciplined,
he should focus his whole mind on me;
when the senses are in his control,

5. INTEREST IN SENSUAL INDULGENCE FALLS AWAY

that man is a man of firm wisdom.

Bhagavad Gita. 2.61.

Buddha:

He who lives without looking for pleasures, his senses well controlled, moderate in his food, faithful and strong, him Māra will certainly not overthrow, any more than the wind throws down a rock mountain.

The Dhammapada. 1.8.

If a man's thoughts are free from lust, if his mind is not perplexed, if he has renounced merit and demerit, then there is no fear from him while he is watchful.

The Dhammapada. 3.39.

Muhammad's Revelation:

And so, set thy face steadfastly towards the [one ever-true] faith, turning away from all that is false, in accordance with the natural disposition which God has instilled into man: [for,] not to allow any change to corrupt what God has thus created— this is the [purpose of the one] ever-true faith; but most people know it not.

The Qur'an. Al-Rum (The Byzantines) 30:30.

SIMPLICITY TESTIMONY 5

Meher Baba:

Though control might be difficult at the beginning, through sincere effort it gradually becomes natural and easy to achieve.

Meher Baba, *Discourses*, 7th edition. P. 49.

Control that has true spiritual value does not consist in the mechanical repression of thoughts and desires, but is the natural restraint exercised by perception of positive values discovered during the process of experience.

Meher Baba, *Discourses*, 7th edition. P. 50.

Only in the gathered silence
    Of a calm and waiting frame
Light and wisdom as from Heaven
    To the seeker came.

Not to ease and aimless quiet
    Doth that inward answer tend,
But to works of love and duty
    As our being's end, –

Not to idle dreams and trances,
    Length of face, and solemn tone,
But to Faith, in daily striving
    And performance shown.

Earnest toil and strong endeavor
    Of a spirit which within
Wrestles with familiar evil
    And besetting sin;

John Greenleaf Whittier, "To ___, With a Copy of Woolman's Journal," in *The Complete Poetical Works of John Greenleaf Whittier*, p 109-111.

SIMPLICITY PRINCIPLE 6

RENUNCIATION

If you renounce for Me everything physical, mental, and spiritual, then you will have Me.

Quakers:

"Away with these whimsicall Narrow Imaginations, and let the Spirit of God which he hath given us, Lead us, & Guide us: And Let us stand fast in that liberty wherewith Christ hath made us free, and not be intangled againe into bondage in observing proscriptions, in outward things which will not profitt, nor cleanse the inward man."

Margaret Fell, *Undaunted Zeal: The Letters of Margaret Fell*, "To Friends, Brethren and Sisters April 1700," p. 470.

I then heard a soft melodious voice, more pure and harmonious than any I had heard with my ears before; I believed it was the voice of an angel who spake to the other angels; the words were "John Wollman is dead." Then the mystery was opened and I perceived there was joy in heaven over a sinner who had repented, and that the language "John Woolman is dead" meant no more than the death of my own will.

John Woolman, *The Journal of John Woolman (HC)*, 1772. P. 306-07.

Jesus:

So likewise, whosoever he be of you that forsaketh not all that

6. RENUNCIATION

he hath, he cannot be my disciple.

Luke 14:33 (KJV).

For they that are after the flesh do mind the things of the flesh; but they that are after the Spirit the things of the Spirit. For to be carnally minded is death; but to be spiritually minded is life and peace.

Romans 8:5-6 (KJV).

Tanakh:

Mark, the tenth day of this seventh month is the Day of Atonement. It shall be a sacred occasion for you: you shall practice self-denial, and you shall bring an offering by fire to the Lord; you shall do no work throughout that day. For it is a Day of Atonement.

Tanakh: The Holy Scriptures. Leviticus 23:27-28.

When My people, who bear My name, humble themselves, pray, and seek My favor and turn from their evil ways, I will hear in My heavenly abode and forgive their sins and heal their land.

Tanakh: The Holy Scriptures. II Chronicles 7:14.

Zarathushtra:

She is indeed our Refuge safe; She brings
Soul-Strength and Life-renewed, twin gifts of Love;
    God hath covered Her with food for man,
    She feedeth all mankind since dawn of Life;

SIMPLICITY TESTIMONY 6

Such is God's Plan—and Knowledge's Law.

The Divine Songs of Zarathushtra. Spenta-Mainyu 2.6—Yasna 48.6.

Krishna:

Calmly renouncing all actions,
the embodied Self dwells at ease
as lord of the nine-gated city,
not acting, not causing action.

Bhagavad Gita. 5.13.

Self-mastered, with mind unattached
at all times, beyond desire,
one attains through renunciation
the supreme freedom from action.

Bhagavad Gita. 18.49.

6. RENUNCIATION

Buddha:

Those whose minds are well-grounded in the (seven) elements of knowledge, who rejoice in the renunciation of affections and in freedom from attachments, whose evil proclivities have been overcome and who are full of light, are completely liberated even in this world.

The Dhammapada. 6:89.

There is no suffering for him who has finished his journey, and abandoned grief, who has freed himself on all sides, and thrown off all fetters.

The Dhammapada. 7:90.

Muhammad's Revelation:

Verily, as for those who have attained to faith [in this divine writ], and those who follow the Jewish faith, and the Sabians, and the Christians, and the Magians, [on the one hand,] and those who are bent on ascribing divinity to aught but God, [on the other,] — verily, God will decide between them on Resurrection Day: for, behold, God is witness unto everything.

The Qur'an. Al-Hajj (The Pilgrimage) 22:17.

And if indeed you are slain or die in God's cause, then surely forgiveness from God and His grace are better than all that one could amass [in this world]: for, indeed, if you die or are slain, it will surely be unto God that you shall be gathered.

The Qur'an. Al-Imran (The House of Imran) 3:157-158.

SIMPLICITY TESTIMONY 6

<u>Meher Baba:</u>

Renunciation of desires does not mean asceticism or a merely negative attitude to life….It is a positive attitude of releasing all that is good, noble, and beautiful in man. It also contributes to all that is gracious and lovely in the environment.

Meher Baba, *Discourses*, 7th edition. P. 15.

Only by treading the path of inner and spontaneous renunciation of craving is it possible to attain true freedom and unity.

Meher Baba, *Discourses*, 7th edition. P. 101.

With that deep insight which detects
    All great things in the small.
And knows how each man's life affects
    The spiritual life of all.
He walked by faith and not by sight,
    By love and not by law;
The presence of the wrong or right
    He rather felt than saw.

He felt that wrong with wrong partakes,
    That nothing stands alone,
That whoso gives the motive, makes
    His brother's sin his own.
And, pausing not for doubtful choice
    Of evils great or small,
He listened to that inward voice
    Which called away from all.

John Greenleaf Whittier, "The Quaker of Olden Time," in *The Complete Poetical Works of John Greenleaf Whittier*, p 98.

SIMPLICITY PRINCIPLE 7

OBEDIENCE TO WHAT YOU KNOW TO BE TRUE

If your obedience is as spontaneous, complete, and natural as light is to the eye or smell is to the nose, then you will come to Me.

Quakers:

"Friends, whose Minds are turn'd to the Light, which comes from Jesus Christ, which never changeth, whose Light enlightens every one coming into the World; in it abide, and in it walk, and to it be faithful and obedient in your Measures, that with it your Minds may be guided up to God, who is the Father of Lights, that you may bring your Deeds to the Light, to try whether they are wrought in God."

Margaret Fell, *Undaunted Zeal: The Letters of Margaret Fell*, "An Epistle to Friends 1653," p. 51.

"My mind in this tempest, through the gracious assistance of the Lord, was preserved in a good degree of resignation, and I felt at times a few words in his love to my shipmates in regard to the all-sufficiency of him who formed the great deep, and whose care is so extensive that a sparrow falls not without his notice, and thus in a tender frame of mind spake to them of the necessity of our yielding in true obedience to the instructions of our Heavenly Father, who sometimes through adversities indendeth our refinement."

John Woolman, *The Journal and Major Essays of John Woolman*, p 169.

7. OBEDIENCE TO WHAT YOU KNOW TO BE TRUE

"Cultivate this ennobling view; be obedient to the truth; so will you make advancement in your several neighborhoods and become wiser than your teachers. You will exalt the standard of justice and mercy above that around which your Fathers have rallied."

Lucretia Mott, *Lucretia Mott Speaks: The Essential Speeches and Sermons*, "'Sermon to the Medical Students, Cherry Street Meeting, Philadelphia, February 11, 1849,'" p. 51.

Jesus:

Then Peter and the other apostles answered and said, We ought to obey God rather than men....And we are his witnesses of these things; and so is also the Holy Ghost, whom God hath given to them that obey him.

Acts 5:29-32 (KJV).

Seeing ye have purified your souls in obeying the truth through the Spirit unto unfeigned love of the brethren, see that ye love one another with a pure heart fervently: Being born again, not of corruptible seed, but of incorruptible, by the word of God, which liveth and abideth for ever.

1 Peter 1:22-23 (KJV).

Tanakh:

"Does the Lord delight in burnt offerings and sacrifices
As much as in obedience to the Lord's command?
Surely, obedience is better than sacrifice,

Compliance than the fat of rams."

Tanakh: The Holy Scriptures. 1 Samuel 15:22.

And now, O Israel, what does the Lord your God demand of you? Only this: to revere the Lord your God, to walk only in His paths, to love Him, and to serve the Lord your God with all your heart and soul, keeping the Lord's commandments and laws.

Tanakh: The Holy Scriptures. Deuteronomy 10:12-13.

<u>Zarathushtra:</u>

Such are, indeed, the Saviours of the Earth,
They follow Duty's call, the call of Love :
God, they listen unto Love;
      They do what Knowledge bids, and Thy Commands;
      Surely they are the Vanquishers of Hate.

The Divine Songs of Zarathushtra. Spenta-Mainyu 2.12—Yasna 48.12.

<u>Krishna:</u>

Those who realize the essence
of duty, who trust me completely
and surrender their lives to me—

I love them with very great love.

Bhagavad Gita. 12.20.

7. OBEDIENCE TO WHAT YOU KNOW TO BE TRUE

Buddha:

Rouse thyself by thyself, examine thyself by thyself; thus self-guarded and mindful, wilt thou, O monk, live happily. For self is the lord of self, self is the refuge of self, therefore curb thyself as the merchant curbs a good horse.

The Dhammapada. 25:379–380.

Muhammad's Revelation:

And His is all that is in the heavens and on earth, and to Him [alone] obedience is always due: will you, then, pay reverence to aught but God?

The Qur'an. An-Nahl (The Bee) 16:52.

The only response of believers, whenever they are summoned unto God and His Apostle in order that [the divine writ] might judge between them, can be no other than, "We have heard, and we pay heed!" – and it is they, they who shall attain to a happy state: for, they who pay heed unto God and His Apostle, and stand in awe of God and are conscious of Him, it is they, they who shall triumph [in the end]!

The Qur'an. An-Nur (The Light) 24:51-52.

Meher Baba:

Literal obedience is the effect of the rocklike faith and deep love that the Master inspires in the pupil through his human appeal.

Meher Baba, Discourses, 7th edition. P. 59.

SIMPLICITY TESTIMONY 7

Through such implicit and unquestioning obedience, all the crooked knots of your desires and sanskaras are set straight. It is also through such obedience that a deep link is created between the Master and the pupil, with the result that there is an unhindered and perennial flow of spiritual wisdom and power into the pupil.

Meher Baba, *Discourses*, 7th edition. P. 59.

SECTION FOUR

TRUTH

One holy name bearing, no longer they need
Credentials of party, and pass-words of creed
The new song they sing hath a threefold accord,
And they own one baptism, one faith, and one Lord!

John Greenleaf Whittier, "Quaker Alumni," in *The Complete Poetical Works of John Greenleaf Whittier*, p 254-258.

TRUTH PRINCIPLE 1

OUR REAL EXISTENCE IS ONENESS

The only Real Existence is that of the One and only God, Who is the Self in every (finite) self.

Quakers:

"So, as you love your Eternal Peace, and the Redemption of your Souls, keep low in your measures of the Living Testimony which cometh from the Living God, which is one in all; in its measure, and there is no Division, nor no Rent, but all one; and this gathers your Hearts together, and this knits and unites unto the Body, where the Unity is;.... So in Love and Tenderness to your Souls, I Warn and Charge you from the Lord, keep in the Light, which is one, in the Power, which is one, in the measure of Life made manifest in you, which is one: And here is no Division, nor Separation, but a gathering and a knitting."

Margaret Fell, *Undaunted Zeal: The Letters of Margaret Fell.* Edited by Elsa F. Glines. "An Epistle to Friends 1655," p. 171.

I saw that Christ enlightens all men and women with His divine and saving Light. I saw that the grace of God, which brings salvation has appeared to all men, and that the manifestation of God was given to every man to profit withal.

George Fox, *The Journal of George Fox*, "A Spiritual Worship," 1649, p. 21.

Therefore I say, preach your Truth; let it go forth, and you will find, without any notable miracle, as of old, that everyone will speak in their own tongue, in which they were born. And I will say that if these pure principles have their

1. OUR REAL EXISTENCE IS ONENESS

place in us and are brought forth by faithfulness and obedience into practice, the difficulties and doubts that we might have to surmount will be easily conquered. There will be a power higher than these. Let it be called The Great Spirit of the Indian, the Quaker's "Inward Light" of George Fox, the blessed "Mary, Mother of Jesus" of the Catholics: or Brahma, the Hindu's God—they will all be one, and there will come to be such faith and such liberty as shall redeem the world.

Lucretia Mott, *Lucretia Mott Speaks: The Essential Speeches and Sermons*, "To the Free Religious Association," 1873, p. 204.

Jesus:

...But to us there is but one God, the Father, of whom are all things, and we in him.

1 Corinthians 8:4–6 (AV).

And Jesus answered him, "The first of all the commandments is, Hear, O Israel; The Lord our God is one Lord: And thou shalt love the Lord thy God with all thy heart, and with all thy soul, and with all thy mind, and with all thy strength: this is the first commandment."

Mark 12:29–30 (AV).

Tanakh:

You will know and believe in Me, and understand that I am He; before Me nothing was created by a god, nor will there be after Me!

Tanach, The Stone Edition. (Brooklyn, NY: Mesorah Publications, Ltd., 2011), Isaiah 43:10.

It has been clearly demonstrated to you that the Lord alone is God; there is none beside Him.

Tanakh: The Holy Scriptures. Deuteronomy 4:35.

Hear, O Israel! The Lord is our God, the Lord alone.

Tanakh: The Holy Scriptures. Deuteronomy 6:4.

Zarathushtra:

All Holy Lives are put into Thy hands,
All that have been, and all that are today,
And all, Oh God, that ever shall be.

The Divine Songs of Zarathushtra, Ahunavaiti 6.10—Yasna 33:10.

Krishna:

I am the Self, Arjuna,
seated in the heart of all beings;
I am the beginning and the life span
of beings, and their end as well.

Bhagavad Gita. 10.20.

1. OUR REAL EXISTENCE IS ONENESS

When he sees that the myriad beings
emanate from the One
and have their source in the One,
that man gains absolute freedom.

This supreme Self is beginningless,
deathless, and unconfined;
although it inhabits bodies,
it neither acts nor is tainted.

Bhagavad Gita. 13.30–31.

Buddha:

Because of Ignorance (avidya) the principle of individuation as discriminated from Enlightenment which is the principle of unity and sameness the primal unity becomes divided into thinking, thinker and discriminated thoughts by reason of which there appear the "formations" of karma.

A Buddhist Bible. p. 645.

Muhammad's Revelation:

All praise is due to God alone, the Sustainer of all the worlds, the Most Gracious, the Dispenser of Grace, Lord of the Day of Judgment! Thee alone do we worship, and unto Thee alone do we turn for aid.

The Qur'an. Al-Fātihah (The Opening) 1:2–5.

This is a message unto all mankind. Hence, let them be warned thereby, and let them know that He is the One and

TRUTH TESTIMONY 1

Only God; and let those who are endowed with insight take this to heart!

The Qur'an. 'Ibrāhīm (Abraham) 14:52.

And unto God belongs all that is in the heavens and all that is on earth; and all things go back to God [as their source].

The Qur'an. Al-Imran (The House of Imran) 3:109.

<u>Meher Baba:</u>

All souls (atmas) were, are and will be in the Over-Soul (Paramatma). Souls (atmas) are all One.

...Most souls have great binding; some souls have little binding; a few souls have very little binding; and a very few souls have absolutely no binding.

All these souls (atmas) of different consciousness, of different experiences, of different states are in the Over-Soul (Paramatma)...and all are One.

Meher Baba, *God Speaks*, 2nd edition. (Walnut Creek, CA: Sufism Reoriented, 1973), pp. 1–2.

But, bowed in lowliness of mind,
>   I make my humble wishes known, –
I only ask a will resigned,
>   O Father, to thine own!

To-day, beneath thy chastening eye
>   I crave alone for peace and rest,
Submissive in thy hand to lie,
>   And feel that it is best.

John Greenleaf Whittier, "The Wish of To-Day," in *The Complete Poetical Works of John Greenleaf Whittier*, p 150.

TRUTH PRINCIPLE 2

LOVE IS LIVING BY SPIRITUAL PRINCIPLES

To love God as He ought to be loved, we must live for God and die for God, knowing that the goal of life is to love God, and find Him as our own Self.

<u>Quakers:</u>

"There is in all religious associations a constant tendency to retrogression. Having begun in the spirit there is a disposition too manifest to seek to be made perfect by the flesh, to go back again to the weak and beggarly elements and to desire, and be willing, to be brought into bondage again. The only way in which we can be preserved from this downward step, from this backsliding, is that we go forward, that we advance, that we follow the light, not that we sit down in listless indolence."

Lucretia Mott, *Lucretia Mott Speaks: The Essential Speeches and Sermons*, "Cherry Street Meeting, Philadelphia, November 6, 1849" p. 64.

"Here I was renewedly confirmed in my mind that the Lord, whose tender mercies are over all his works and whose ear is open to the cries and groans of the oppressed, is graciously moving on the hearts of people to draw them off from the desire of wealth and bring them into such a humble, lowly way of living that they may see their way clearly to repair to the standard of true righteousness, and not only break the yoke of oppression, but know him to be their strength and support in a time of outward affliction."

John Woolman, *The Journal and Major Essays of John Woolman*, p 148.

2. LOVE IS LIVING BY SPIRITUAL PRINCIPLES

Jesus:

But if any man love God, the same is known of him.

1 Corinthians 8:3 (AV).

Beloved, let us love one another: for love is of God; and every one that loveth is born of God, and knoweth God. He that loveth not knoweth not God; for God is love.

1 John 4:7–8 (AV).

Tanakh:

You shall love the Lord your God with all your heart and with all your soul and with all your might.

Tanakh: The Holy Scriptures. Deuteronomy 6:5.

But be very careful to fulfill the Instruction and the Teaching that Moses the servant of the Lord enjoined upon you, to love the Lord your God and to walk in all His ways, and to keep His commandments and hold fast to Him, and to serve Him with all your heart and soul.

Tanakh: The Holy Scriptures. Joshua 22:5.

Zarathushtra:

He, through His Holy Word, did first declare,
    His LIGHT shall stream through all the Lights on high;
Himself, All-Wise, the Law of Truth declared,
    That this His LIGHT might glow as LOVE Supreme;
Make it blaze higher, God, through the grace
    Of Thine own Spirit, evermore the same.

The Divine Songs of Zarathushtra. Ahunavaiti 4.7—Yasna 31.7.

Thus may I realise Thee as the First
    And also Last, O God, in my mind,
    As Father of all LOVE—of Love;
Thus may I ever hold Thee in mine eye,
    As the true Parent of ETERNAL LAW,
    As Judge Supreme of every act of man.

The Divine Songs of Zarathushtra. Ahunavaiti 4.8—Yasna 31.8.

Krishna:

Concentrate your mind on me,
fill your heart with my presence,
love me, serve me, worship me,
and you will attain me at last.

Bhagavad Gita. 9.34.

2. LOVE IS LIVING BY SPIRITUAL PRINCIPLES

Whatever you do, Arjuna,
do it as an offering to me—
whatever you say or eat
or pray or enjoy or suffer.

Bhagavad Gita. 9.27.

Buddha:

Hence, the purpose of the Holy Life does not consist in acquiring alms, honour, or fame, nor in gaining morality, concentration, or the eye of knowledge. That unshakable deliverance of the heart: that, verily, is the object of the Holy Life, that is the essence, that is the goal.

A Buddhist Bible. P. 59–60.

Muhammad's Revelation:

And God endows those who avail themselves of [His] guidance with an ever-deeper consciousness of the right way; and good deeds, the fruit whereof endures forever, are, in thy Sustainer's sight, of far greater merit [than any worldly goods], and yield far better returns.

The Qur'an. Marayam (Mary) 19:76.

God wants to make [all this] clear unto you, and to guide you onto the [righteous] ways of life of those who preceded you, and to turn unto you in His mercy: for God is all-knowing, wise. And God wants to turn unto you in His mercy, whereas those who follow [only] their own lusts want you to drift far away from the right path. God wants to lighten your burdens:

TRUTH TESTIMONY 2

for man has been created weak.

The Qur'an. An-Nisaa (Women) 4:26-28.

Meher Baba:

God is worth living for, and He is also worth dying for. All else is a vain and empty pursuit of illusory values.

Meher Baba, *Discourses*, 7th edition. P. 339.

Divine love is unlimited in essence and expression because it is experienced by the soul through the Soul itself.... Divine love is entirely free from the thralldom of desires or the limiting self. In this state of Infinity the lover has no being apart from the Beloved: he is the Beloved Himself.

Meher Baba, *Discourses*, 7th edition. P. 402–403.

The autumn-time has come;
On woods that dream of bloom,
And over purpling vines,
The low sun fainter shines.

The aster-flower is failing,
The hazel's gold is paling;
Yet overhead more near
The eternal stars appear!

And present gratitude
Insures the future's good,
And for the things I see
I trust the things to be;

That in the paths untrod,
And the long days of God,
My feet shall still be led,
My heart be comforted.

John Greenleaf Whittier, "My Triumph," in *The Complete Poetical Works of John Greenleaf Whittier*, p 351-352.

TRUTH PRINCIPLE 3

REMEMBER GOD WITH YOUR DYING BREATH

What you think of every day is what you will remember with your dying breath.

Quakers:

"— And Deare Friends, I am not uncensible; of your great Care, & service for the Lord, and his Etternall Truth; Therefore I Councell you, in the power of the Lord, to continue in it and to give upp freely to it, in the strength & wisdom of God; and you are sure to have comfort & satisfaction at the present, and in the End, an Everlasting & Etternall Reward."

Margaret Fell, *Undaunted Zeal: The Letters of Margaret Fell*, "To Friends and Sisters November 19, 1691," p. 454.

"To forward this work the all-wise God is sometimes pleased through outward distress to bring us near the gates of death, that life being painful and afflicting and the prospect of eternity open before us, all earthly bonds may be loosened and the mind prepared for that deep and sacred instruction which otherwise would not be received."

John Woolman, *The Journal and Major Essays of John Woolman*, p.56.

Jesus:

And when Jesus had cried with a loud voice, he said, Father, into thy hands I commend my spirit: and having said thus, he gave up the ghost. Now when the centurion saw what was done, he

3. REMEMBER GOD WITH YOUR DYING BREATH

glorified God, saying, Certainly this was a righteous man.

Luke 23:46-47 (KJV).

For whosoever shall call upon the name of the Lord shall be saved.

Romans 10:13-15 (KJV).

Tanakh:

But let all who take refuge in You rejoice,
    ever jubilant as You shelter them;
    and let those who love Your name exult in You.
For You surely bless the righteous man, O Lord,
    encompassing him with favor like a shield.

Tanakh: The Holy Scriptures. Psalms 5:12–13.

You shall love the Lord your God with all your heart and with all your soul and with all your might. Take to heart these instructions with which I charge you this day. Impress them upon your children. Recite them when you stay at home and when you are away, when you lie down and when you get up. Bind them as a sign on your hand and let them serve as a symbol on your forehead; inscribe them on the doorposts of your house and on your gates.

Tanakh: The Holy Scriptures. Deuteronomy 6:5-9.

Zarathushtra:

And if some be, who in their Righteousness,
    And by their Loving Hearts appear to Thee,

TRUTH TESTIMONY 3

> As truly-seeing and upright, O Lord,
> Grant them in full all that their Souls desire;
> For I believe no pray'r devout for Truth
> Can e'er remain unanswered from Your side.

The Divine Songs of Zarathushtra. Ahunavaiti 2.10—Yasna 28.10.

Krishna:

Whoever in his final moments
thinks of me only, is sure
to enter my state of being
once his body is dead.

Bhagavad Gita. 8.5.

If you do this at the hour of your death,
with an unmoving mind, drawing
your breath up between your eyebrows,
you will reach the Person that I am.

Bhagavad Gita. 8.10.

Buddha:

He who takes refuge with Buddha, the Law and the Order; he who with clear understanding sees the four noble truths: – Suffering, the origin of suffering, the destruction of suffering, and the eightfold noble path that leads to the release from suffering – That is the safe refuge, that is the best refuge; having gone to

3. REMEMBER GOD WITH YOUR DYING BREATH

that refuge, a man is delivered from all suffering.

The Dhammapada. 14:190–192.

Muhammad's Revelation:

Say: "Invoke God, or invoke the Most Gracious: by whichever name you invoke Him, [He is always the One – for] His are all the attributes of perfection."

The Qur'an. Al-ʾIsrāaʾ (The Night Journey) 17:110.

"Verily, I – I alone – am God; there is no deity save Me. Hence, worship Me alone, and be constant in prayer, so as to remember Me!"

The Qur'an. Tā Hā (O Man) 20:14.

Meher Baba:

Thus a person who is not very learned but who sincerely takes the name of God and does his humble duties wholeheartedly may actually be nearer to God than one who knows all the metaphysics of the world but does not allow any of his theories to modify his everyday life.

Meher Baba, *Discourses*, 7th edition. P. 262.

TRUTH TESTIMONY 3

I feel the unutterable longing,
    Thy hunger of the heart is mine;
I reach and grope for hands in darkness,
    My ear grows sharp for voice or sign.

Still on the lips of all we question
    The finger of God's silence lies;
Will the lost hands in ours be folded?
    Will the shut eyelids ever rise?

O friend! no proof beyond this yearning,
    This outreach of our hearts, we need;
God will not mock the hope He giveth,
    No love He prompts shall vainly plead.

John Greenleaf Whittier, "To Lydia Maria Child, On Reading Her Poem in 'The Standard,'" in *The Complete Poetical Works of John Greenleaf Whittier*, p 353-354.

TRUTH PRINCIPLE 4

LONGING FOR TRUTH AND UNION

If you experience that same longing and thirst for union with Me as one who has been lying for days in the hot sun of the Sahara experiences the longing for water, then you will realize Me.

Quakers:

"In the everlastinge Fountaine of life, where the Covenant stands I am one with thee, where there is fullness of joy & peace for evermore, And veryly my love to thee is inexpressable Neither can pen write, but where the Spirritt of the liveing God unites, where there is noe separation, but presence one with Another, there tread my dear brother, where noe persecution touches, where no vulterous eye nor venomous beast shall ever come, oh here, here dwells my owne deare heart, where the Redemption is....".

Margaret Fell, *Undaunted Zeal: The Letters of Margaret Fell*, "To William Dewsbury August 14, 1655," p. 139

From the time of my entering Maryland I have been much under sorrow, which of late so increased upon me that my mind was almost overwhelmed, and I may say with the Psalmist, "In my distress I called upon the Lord and cried to my God" [Ps. 18:6], who in infinite goodness looked upon my affliction and in my private retirement sent the Comforter for my relief, for which I humbly bless his holy name.

John Woolman, *The Journal and Major Essays of John Woolman*, p 64.

4. LONGING FOR TRUTH AND UNION

Jesus:

Blessed are they which do hunger and thirst after righteousness: for they shall be filled."

Matthew 5:6 (KJV).

Jesus answered and said unto her, Whosoever drinketh of this water shall thirst again: But whosoever drinketh of the water that I shall give him shall never thirst; but the water that I shall give him shall be in him a well of water springing up into everlasting life.

John 4:13-15 (KJV).

Tanakh:

My soul is consumed with longing
For Your rules at all times.

Tanakh: The Holy Scriptures. Psalms 119:20.

God, You are my God;
    I search for You,
    my soul thirsts for You,
    my body yearns for You,
    as a parched and thirsty land that has no water.

Tanakh: The Holy Scriptures. Psalms 63:2.

TRUTH TESTIMONY 4

<u>Zarathushtra:</u>

As Thy true worshipper, in Knowledge firm,
      With all my heart, Thy Spirit Holiest
      For His protecting grace do I invoke;
I will fulfil the guardianship He planned;
      So, God, I would ask of Thee
      A vision of Thyself and speech with Thee.

The Divine Songs of Zarathushtra. Ahunavaiti 6.6—Yasna 33.6.

<u>Krishna:</u>

He who faithfully serves me
with the yoga of devotion, going
beyond the three gunas, is ready
to attain the ultimate freedom.

Bhagavad Gita. 14.26.

<u>Buddha:</u>

He in whom a desire for the Ineffable has sprung up, whose mind is permeated by this desire and whose thoughts are not bewildered by sensuality, is said to be 'bound up-stream.'

The Dhammapada. 16:218.

4. LONGING FOR TRUTH AND UNION

<u>Muhammad's Revelation:</u>

O Mankind! Worship your Sustainer, who has created you and those who lived before you, so that you might remain conscious of Him who has made the earth a resting-place for you and the sky a canopy, and has sent down water from the sky and thereby brought forth fruits for your sustenance: do not, then, claim that there is any power that could rival God, when you know [that He is One].

The Qur'an. Al-Baqarah (The Cow) 2:21–22.

<u>Meher Baba:</u>

Open your heart by weeding out all desires and by harboring only one longing—the longing for union with the ultimate Reality.

Meher Baba, *Discourses*, 7th edition. P. 14.

As the fish that is taken out of the water longs to go back in the water, the aspirant who has perceived the goal longs to be united with God.

Meher Baba, *Discourses*, 7th edition. P. 128.

TRUTH TESTIMONY 4

That death seems but a covered way
    Which opens into light,
Wherein no blinded child can stray
    Beyond the Father's sight; –

That care and trial seem at last,
    Through Memory's sunset air,
Like mountain-ranges overpast,
    In purple distance fair; –

That all the jarring notes of life
    Seem blending in a psalm,
And all the angles of its strife
    Slow rounding into calm.

John Greenleaf Whittier, "My Psalm," in *The Complete Poetical Works of John Greenleaf Whittier*, p 242-243.

TRUTH PRINCIPLE 5

DESPERATION/PASSION

If you experience the desperation that causes a person to commit suicide and you feel that you cannot live without seeing Me, then you will see Me.

Quakers:

"We should all be filled with this spirit which shall desire the universal spread of peace on earth and goodwill among men. Let it be regarded as a zeal without knowledge, though you may be accused of being over zealously affected. I tell you nay, it is good to be zealously affected in a good cause, and I rejoice in the great efforts that are being made for the spread of true principles and the carrying of them out in our intercourse with our fellow beings."

Lucretia Mott, *Lucretia Mott Speaks: The Essential Speeches and Sermons*, "Cherry Street Meeting, Philadelphia, November 6, 1849," p. 66.

"In the year 1648, as I was sitting in a Friend's house in Nottinghamshire (for by this time the power of God had opened the hearts of some to receive the word of life and reconciliation) I saw there was a great crack to go throughout the earth, and a great smoke to go as the crack went; and that after the crack there should be great shaking: this was the earth in people's hearts, which was to be shaken before the seed of God was raised out of the earth. And it was so; for the Lord's power began to shake them, and great meetings we began to have, and a mighty power and work of God there was amongst people, to

5. DEPRESSION/PASSION

the astonishment of both people and priests."

George Fox, *The Journal of George Fox*, "Outward and Inward Law," 1648, p.13.

From my early acquaintance with Truth I have often felt an inward distress occasioned by the striving of a spirit in me against the operation of the Heavenly Principle, and in this circumstance have been affected with a sense of my own wretchedness, and in a mourning condition felt earnest longings for that divine help which brings the soul into true liberty.

John Woolman, *The Journal and Major Essays of John Woolman*, p. 119.

Jesus:

"Blessed are they which do hunger and thirst after righteousness: for they shall be filled."

Matthew 5:6 (AV).

Tanakh:

Like a hind crying for water,
    my soul cries for You, O God;
    my soul thirsts for God, the living God;
    O when will I come to appear before God!
My tears have been my food day and night;
    I am ever taunted with, "Where is your God?"
When I think of this, I pour out my soul.

Tankah: The Holy Scriptures. Psalms 42:2-5.

At night I yearn for You with all my being,
I seek You with all the spirit within me.

Tanakh: The Holy Scriptures. Isaiah 26:9.

Zarathushtra:

This do I ask, God, tell me true:
Reveal Thy purpose, God, for my Soul;
> I seek Thy Teachings true through Love,
> Through Knowledge's Wisdom seek the Goal of Life;
> With all my Soul Thy orders I'll obey,
> And thus attain Thee and Eternal Light.

The Divine Songs of Zarathushtra. Ustavaiti 2.8—Yasna 44.8.

Krishna:

Those who love and revere me
With unwavering faith, always
Centering their minds on me—
They are the most perfect in yoga.

Bhagavad Gita. 12.2.

Concentrate every thought
on me alone; with a mind
fully absorbed, one-pointed,
you will live within me, forever.

Bhagavad Gita. 12.8.

5. DEPRESSION/PASSION

Buddha:

The Lord Buddha continued: — Subhuti, should there be any good pious disciple, man or woman, who in his zeal to practice charity is willing to sacrifice his life in the morning, or at noontide, or in the evening, on as many occasions as there are grains of sand in the river Ganges, even if these occasions recur for a hundred thousand myriad kalpas, would his blessing and merit be great? It would be great indeed, Lord Buddha.

A Buddhist Bible. P. 96.

Muhammad's Revelation:

Their parable is that of people who kindle a fire: but as soon as it has illumined all around them, God takes away their light and leaves them in utter darkness, wherein they cannot see: deaf, dumb, blind — and they cannot turn back. Or [the parable] of a violent cloudburst in the sky, with utter darkness, thunder and lightning: they put their fingers into their ears to keep out the peals of thunder, in terror of death.

The Qur'an. Al-Baqarah (The Cow) 2:17-19.

Meher Baba:

Divine desperateness is the beginning of spiritual awakening because it gives rise to the aspiration for God-realization.

Meher Baba, *Discourses*, 7th edition. P. 126.

TRUTH TESTIMONY 5

When the mental energy of an individual is thus centered upon discovering the goal of life, he uses the power of desperateness creatively.

Meher Baba, *Discourses*, 7th edition. P. 126.

Know well, my soul, God's hand controls
    Whate'er thou fearest;
Round him in calmest music rolls
    Whate'er thou hearest.

What to thee is shadow, to him is day,
    And the end he knoweth,
And not on a blind and aimless way
    The spirit goeth.

Man sees no future, – a phantom show
    Is alone before him:
Past Time is dead, and the grasses grow,
    And flowers bloom o'er him.

Nothing before, nothing behind;
    The steps of Faith
Fall on the seeming void, and find
    The rock beneath.

John Greenleaf Whittier, "My Soul and I," in *The Complete Poetical Works of John Greenleaf Whittier*, p 92-95.

TRUTH PRINCIPLE 6

FAITH

If you have the complete faith that Kalyan had in his Master—in believing it was night although it was day because his Master said so—then you will know Me.

Quakers:

"And so my dearly beloved Friends, in the Bowels of tender and hearty Love, do I desire and beseech you, to be true and faithful to the Lord God, and to his Truth, and to your own Souls in this his Day, which may be a Day of Tryal; for Satan desires to winnow and sift you; but blessed are you, whose Faith fails not, but abides the fiery Tryal, which is to try every one's Faith; and the Faith which is tried, is much more Precious than Gold that perisheth."

Margaret Fell, *Undaunted Zeal: The Letters of Margaret Fell*, "An Epistle to Friends June 7, 1664," p. 378.

"...and by faith yee stand, soe in the faith continue firme and steadfast, and bee not tossed too and froe, neither wandering, but in the unity of the Faith of gods elect all stand, and all waite[,] building up on another in your most holy faith, for the Lord preserveth the faithfull[,] mine eyes shall bee upon the faithfull [Ps. 101:6] saith the Lord."

Margaret Fell, *Undaunted Zeal: The Letters of Margaret Fell*, "To Brethren and Sisters 1658," p. 261.

I awoke; it was yet dark, and no appearance of day or moonshine, and as I opened mine eyes I saw a light in my chamber, at the apparent distance of five feet, about nine inches in diameter, of a clear easy brightness, and near its centre the most radiant. As I lay still looking upon it without any surprise, words were spoken to my inward ear, which filled my whole inward man. They were not the effect of thought, nor any conclusion in relation to the appearance, but as the language of the Holy One spoken in my mind. The words were CERTAIN EVIDENCE OF DIVINE TRUTH. They were again repeated exactly in the same manner, and then the light disappeared.

John Woolman, *The Journal of John Woolman (HC)*, 1758, p. 200.

Jesus:

And Jesus said unto them,...If ye have faith as a grain of mustard seed, ye shall say unto this mountain, Remove hence to yonder place; and it shall remove; and nothing shall be impossible unto you.

Matthew 17:20 (KJV).

Now faith is the substance of things hoped for, the evidence of things not seen.... Through faith we understand that the worlds were framed by the word of God, so that things which are seen were not made of things which do appear.

Hebrews 11:1-3 (KJV).

Tanakh:

Trust in the Lord with all your heart,
And do not rely on your own understanding.
In all your ways acknowledge Him,

And He will make your paths smooth.

Tanakh: The Holy Scriptures. Proverbs 3:5-6.

Be strong and resolute, be not in fear or in dread...; for the Lord your God Himself marches with you: He will not fail you or forsake you.

Tanakh: The Holy Scriptures. Deuteronomy 31:6.

Zarathushtra:

I'll speak about the Greatest One of All,
Praising Him, Lord of Wisdom through His Truth,
And all the Lords of Wisdom that are His;
    May He through His Good Spirit hear our call,
    Through Love my Faith to Him I pledge,
    He in His Wisdom guides me to His Light.

The Divine Songs of Zarathushtra. Ustavaiti 3.6—Yasna 45.6.

Krishna:

Concentrate your mind on me,
fill your heart with my presence,
love me, serve me, worship me,
and you will attain me at last.

Bhagavad Gita. 9.34.

Those who love and revere me
with unwavering faith, always
centering their minds on me—

6. FAITH

they are the most perfect in yoga.

Bhagavad Gita. 12.2.

Buddha:

Whoso pays homage to those who deserve homage, whether the Awakened or their disciples, those who have overcome the hosts of evils and crossed the flood of sorrow, who have found deliverance and know no fear — his merit can never be measured by anyone.

The Dhammapada. 14:195, 196.

The disciples of Gotama are always wide awake and watchful, and their thoughts day and night are ever set on Buddha.

The Dhammapada. 21:296.

Muhammad's Revelation:

God is near unto those who have faith, taking them out of deep darkness into the light - whereas near unto those who are bent on denying the truth are the powers of evil that take them out of the light into darkness deep.

The Qur'an. Al-Baqarah (The Cow) 2:257.

Verily, those who have attained to faith [in this divine writ], as well as those who follow the Jewish faith, and the Christians, and the Sabians – all whom believe in God and the Last Day and do righteous deeds – shall have their reward with their Sus tainer; and no fear need they have, and neither shall they grieve.

The Qur'an. Al-Baqarah (The Cow) 2:62.

Meher Baba:

The overflowing radiance of the Master's halo and the effulgence of his purity and compassion are mainly responsible for creating in the pupil an unswerving faith, which prepares him to follow the Master's orders implicitly—irrespective of their satisfying his critical spirit.

Meher Baba, *Discourses*, 7th edition. P. 59.

Complete self-surrender and unquestioning love become possible when the disciple achieves unswerving faith in the Master. Faith in the Master is an indispensable part of true discipleship.

Meher Baba, *Discourses*, 7th edition. P. 148.

As thou hast made thy world without,
>   Make thou more fair my world within;
Shine through its lingering clouds of doubt;
>   Rebuke its haunting shapes of sin;
Fill, brief or long, my granted span
Of life with love to thee and man;
Strike when thou wilt the hour of rest,
But let my last days be my best!

John Greenleaf Whittier, "The Clear Vision," in *The Complete Poetical Works of John Greenleaf Whittier*, p 331-332.

TRUTH PRINCIPLE 7

SURRENDER WHOLEHEARTEDLY AND WITHOUT FEAR

If your surrenderance to Me is as wholehearted as that of one who, suffering from insomnia, surrenders to sudden sleep without fear of being lost, then you will have Me.

Quakers:

"Oh ye who are not of any denomination, whose aspirations to God do nevertheless ascend with a confidence in the impartiality of the arm of his protecting power, it will not be by your outward profession but by your works of righteousness that you will show forth your faith; if you yield yourselves to him, and are willing to know his ability — his glorious attributes — he will know you also — he will set you above all the scoffs and frowns of the world."

Lucretia Mott, *Lucretia Mott Speaks: The Essential Speeches and Sermons*, "Unitarian Church, Washington D.C., January 15, 1843," p. 22.

"I remembered that thou art omnipotent, that I had called thee Father, and I felt that I loved thee, and was made quiet in thy will, and I waited for deliverance from thee; thou hadst pity upon me when no man could help me; I saw that meekness under suffering was shown to us in the most affecting example of thy Son, and thou taught me to follow him, and I said, 'Thy will, O Father be done.'"

John Woolman's last words, 1772, *The Journal of John Woolman (HC)*. P. 314.

7. SURRENDER WHOLEHEARTEDLY AND WITHOUT FEAR

Jesus:

If any man will come after me, let him deny himself and take up his cross and follow me. For whosoever will save his life shall lose it: and whosoever will lose his life for my sake will find it.

Matthew 16:24-26 (KJV).

Tanakh:

Now do not be stiff necked like your fathers; submit yourselves to the Lord and come to His sanctuary, which He consecrated forever, and serve the Lord your God ... for the Lord your God is gracious and merciful; He will not turn His face from you if you return to Him.

Tanakh: The Holy Scripture. 2 Chronicles 30:8–9.

"Yet even now"—says the Lord—
"Turn back to Me with all your hearts,
And with fasting, weeping, and lamenting."
Rend your hearts
Rather than your garments,
And turn back to the Lord your God.
For He is gracious and compassionate,
Slow to anger, abounding in kindness,
And renouncing punishment.

Tanakh: The Holy Scriptures. Joel 2:12-13.

TRUTH TESTIMONY 7

<u>Zarathushtra:</u>

But, God, he who through the urge of heart,
Through sacrifice of Self, doth link himself,
And his own Inner Self with Love,
      Finds Wisdom, and Knowledge's Wisdom, too;
        Sheltered by Righteousness, he shall dwell with Them.

The Divine Songs of Zarathushtra. Spenta-Mainyu 3.5—Yasna 49.5.

<u>Krishna:</u>

Surrendering all thoughts of outcome,
unperturbed, self-reliant,
he does nothing at all, even
when fully engaged in actions.

Bhagavad Gita. 4.20.

Those who realize the essence
of duty, who trust me completely
and surrender their lives to me—
I love them with very great love.

Bhagavad Gita. 12.20.

7. SURRENDER WHOLEHEARTEDLY AND WITHOUT FEAR

Buddha:

His thought is quiet, quiet are his words and deed, when he has obtained freedom by true knowledge, when he has thus become a quiet man.

The Dhammapada. 7:96.

Muhammad's Revelation:

Yea, indeed: everyone who surrenders his whole being unto God, and is a doer of good withal, shall have his reward with his Sustainer; and all such need have no fear, and neither shall they grieve.

The Qur'an. Al-Baqarah (The Cow) 2:112.

Behold the only [true] religion in the sight of God is [man's] self-surrender unto Him;...Thus, [O Prophet,] if they argue with thee, say, "I have surrendered my whole being unto God, and [so have] all who follow me!" – and ask those who have been vouchsafed revelation aforetime, as well as all unlettered people, "Have you [too] surrendered yourself unto Him?" And if they surrender themselves unto Him, they are on the right path.

The Qur'an. ʾĀl-ʿImrān (The House of ʿImrān) 3:19–20.

Meher Baba:

Complete self-surrender and unquestioning love become possible when the disciple achieves unswerving faith in the Master.

Meher Baba, *Discourses*, 7th edition. P. 148.

TRUTH TESTIMONY 7

Spiritual advancement is a succession of one surrender after another until the goal of the final surrenderance of the separate ego-life is completely achieved.... Therefore, in a sense, the most complete surrender to the Master is equivalent to the attainment of the Truth, which is the ultimate goal of all spiritual advancement.

Meher Baba, *Discourses*, 7th edition. P. 257.

SECTION FIVE

ORDER

And what is He? – The ripe grain nods,
The sweet dews fall, the sweet flowers blow;
   But darker signs his presence show :
The earthquake and the storm are God's,
   And good and evil interflow.

O hearts of love! O souls that turn
   Like sunflowers to the pure and best!
   To you the truth is manifest :
For they the mind of Christ discern
   Who lean like John upon his breast!

In him of whom the sibyl told,
   For whom the prophet's harp was toned,
   Whose need the sage and magian owned,
The loving heart of God behold,
   The hope for which the ages groaned!

John Greenleaf Whittier, "The Over-Heart," in *The Complete Poetical Works of John Greenleaf Whittier*, p 237-238.

ORDER PRINCIPLE 1

LOVE IS THE LONGING TO KNOW MORE AND IMPROVE OURSELVES

The only Real Love is the Love for this Infinity (God), which arouses an intense longing to see, know, and become one with its Truth (God).

Quakers:

"Oh that we understood the attributes of deity! We should not be speculating upon abstract theory and contending about abstruse doctrines. Would that we understood the attributes of his goodness. He is ever unfolding himself to men, and as they obey his voice, they will be led by his spirit of which all men are endowed with a portion; and as we are thus taught, and cease to look unto man for that instruction which God alone can impart, he will give us an earnest of a better inheritance. Then shall we know that we are all upon equal grounds as regards what we shall do. Let us seek then to secure unto ourselves that which passeth the understanding of man, an inheritance that fadeth not away, even an earnestness of the rock of the glorious covenant where the Lord God enlighteneth the peaceful spirit in the highest is the light thereof."

Lucretia Mott, *Lucretia Mott Speaks: The Essential Speeches and Sermons*, "Unitarian Church, Washington D.C., January 15, 1843," p. 26.

"It is, however, our duty and what concerns us individually, as creatures accountable to our Creator, to employ rightly the understanding which he hath given us, in humbly endeavouring to be acquainted with his will concerning us and with the nature

1. LOVE IS THE LONGING TO KNOW MORE

and tendency of those things which we practice."

John Woolman, The Journal and Major Essays of John Woolman, p. 212.

Jesus:

Jesus said unto him, "Thou shalt love the Lord thy God with all thy heart, and with all thy soul, and with all thy mind. This is the first and great commandment. And the second is like unto it, Thou shalt love thy neighbour as thyself. On these two commandments hang all the law and the prophets."

Matthew 22:37–40 (AV).

"He that hath my commandments, and keeps them, he it is that loveth me: and he that loveth me shall be loved by my Father, and I will love him, and will manifest myself to him."

John 14:21 (AV).

Tanakh:

[God continues:] And I have loved you with an eternal love, therefore I have extended kindness to you.

Tanach, The Stone Edition. Jeremiah 31:2.

To be sure, they seek Me daily,
Eager to learn My ways.
Like a nation that does what is right,
That has not abandoned the laws of its God,
They ask Me for the right way,

ORDER TESTIMONY 1

They are eager for the nearness of God.

Tanakh: The Holy Scriptures. Isaiah 58:2.

Zarathushtra:

Led by the Holy Spirit to the Best,
His tongue shall utter only words of Love.

The Divine Songs of Zarathushtra. Spenta-Mainyu 1.2—Yasna 47.2.

Through Knowledge's Wisdom grant me Inner Strength,
And all-embracing Love through Love.

The Divine Songs of Zarathushtra. Ahunavaiti 6:12—Yasna 33:12.

Krishna:

Whoever, clear-minded, knows me
as the Ultimate Person, knows
all that is truly worth knowing,
and he loves me with all his heart.

Bhagavad Gita. 15.19.

Concentrate your mind on me,
fill your heart with my presence,
love me, serve me, worship me,

1. LOVE IS THE LONGING TO KNOW MORE

and you will attain me at last.

Bhagavad Gita. 9.34.

Buddha:

Whether we see it or fail to see it, it is manifest always and everywhere....
Take your stand on this, and the rest will follow of its own accord;
To trust in the Heart is the Not Two, the Not Two is to trust in the Heart.
I have spoken, but in vain; for what can words tell
Of things that have no yesterday, tomorrow or today?

Buddhist Texts Through the Ages, Edward Conze, ed. Attributed to Takakusu XLVIII, 376, translated by Arthur Waley. (New York: Philosophical Library, 1954), pp. 297–298.

Muhammad's Revelation:

Verily, those who attain to faith and do righteous deeds will the Most Gracious endow with love: and only to this end have we made this [divine writ] easy to understand, in thine own tongue, [O Prophet,] so that thou might convey thereby a glad tiding to the God-conscious.

The Qu'ran. Marayam (Mary) 19:96–97.

Meher Baba:

The sojourn of the soul is a thrilling divine romance in which the lover—who in the beginning is conscious of nothing but emptiness, frustration, superficiality, and the gnawing chains of bondage—gradually attains an increasingly fuller and freer expression of love. And ultimately the lover disappears and merges in the divine Beloved to realize the unity of the lover and the Beloved in the supreme and eternal fact of God as infinite Love.

Meher Baba, *Discourses*, 7th edition. p. 403.

My heart was heavy, for its trust had been
Abused, its kindness answered with foul wrong;
So, turning gloomily from my fellowmen
One summer Sabbath day I strolled among
The green mounds of the village burial place;
Where, pondering how all human love and hate
Find one sad level; and how, soon or late,
Wronged and wrongdoer, each with meekened face,
And cold hands folded over a still heart,
Pass the green threshold of our common grave,
Whither all footsteps tend, whence none depart,
Awed for myself, and pitying my race,
Our common sorrow, like a might wave,
Swept all my pride away, and trembling I forgave!

John Greenleaf Whittier, "Forgiveness," in *The Complete Poetical Works of John Greenleaf Whittier*, p 121.

ORDER PRINCIPLE 2

KNOWLEDGE IS EQUALITY AND NONJUDGEMENT

The only Real Knowledge is the Knowledge that God is the inner dweller in good people and so-called bad, in saint and so-called sinner. This Knowledge requires you to help all equally as circumstances demand, without expectation of reward, and when compelled to take part in a dispute, to act without the slightest trace of enmity or hatred; to try to make others happy with brotherly or sisterly feeling for each one; to harm no one in thought, word, or deed, not even those who harm you.

Quakers:

"I believe man is created innately good; that his instincts are for good. It is by a perversion of these, through disobedience, that the purity of his soul becomes sullied. Rejecting, then, the doctrine of human depravity, denying that by nature we have wicked hearts, I have every confidence, every hope, in addressing an audience of unsophisticated minds, that they may be reached, because I know that the love of God has previously touched their hearts; that He has implanted there, a sense of justice and mercy, of charity and all goodness. This is the beauty and divinity of true religion, that it is universal. Wherever man is found, these great attributes of Deity are there found — a nice sense of justice, a quick perception of love, a keen apprehension of mercy, and of all the glorious attributes of God; without puzzling the mind with attempts to reconcile His imagined infinite justice, with his prescience or his infinite power."

Lucretia Mott, *Lucretia Mott Speaks: The Essential Speeches and Sermons*, "'Sermon to the Medical Students, Cherry Street Meeting, Philadelphia, February 11, 1849,'" p. 49-50.

2. KNOWLEDGE IS EQUALITY AND NONJUDGEMENT

"Would God this Divine Virtue were more implanted and diffused among mankind, the pretenders to Christianity especially, and we should certainly mind piety more than controversy, and exercise Love and Compassion instead of censuring and persecuting one another in any manner whatsoever."

William Penn, *More Fruits of Solitude*, "Of Charity," 1682. (Boston, Massachusetts: Harvard Press, 1927), p. 395.

Jesus:

"This is my commandment, That ye love one another, as I have loved you. Greater love hath no man than this, that a man lay down his life for his friends."

John 15:12–13 (AV).

He that loveth his brother abideth in the light, and there is none occasion of stumbling in him.

1 John 2:10 (AV).

Tanakh:

The spirit of the Lord shall alight upon him:
A spirit of wisdom and insight,
A spirit of counsel and valor,
A spirit of devotion and reverence for the Lord.
He shall sense the truth by his reverence for the Lord:
He shall not judge by what his eyes behold,
Nor decide by what his ears perceive.
This he shall judge the poor with equity

And decide with justice for the lowly of the land.

Tanakh: The Holy Scriptures. Isaiah 11:2-4.

There shall be one law for the citizen and for the stranger who dwells among you.

Tanakh: The Holy Scriptures. Exodus 12:49.

Zarathushtra:

Whatever deeds or words lift up the Mind
Or lower it,—the Self shall follow sure;—
> The choice once made, the Inner Will accepts
> The Mind as guide, for better or for worse;
> Thy Wisdom makes their destinies distinct.

The Divine Songs of Zarathushtra. Spenta-Mainyu 2.4—Yasna 48.4.

Krishna:

When he sees all beings as equal
in suffering or in joy
because they are like himself,
that man has grown perfect in yoga.

Bhagavad Gita. 6.32.

He who sees that the great Lord
is equally in all beings,

2. KNOWLEDGE IS EQUALITY AND NONJUDGEMENT

deathless when every being
dies—that man sees truly.

Bhagavad Gita. 13.27.

Buddha:

As the mind progresses towards Enlightenment, it becomes aware of clearing insight and sensitiveness as to the essential unity of all animate life, and there awakens within him a great heart of compassion and sympathy drawing all animate life together, harmonizing differences, unifying all dualisms.

The Buddhist Bible. P. 653.

There is no path through the air; no (true) monk is found outside (the Buddhist Order). Nought in the phenomenal world abides, but the Awakened (the Buddhas) are never shaken.

The Dhammapada. 18:255.

Muhammad's Revelation:

Unto every community have We appointed [different] ways of worship, which they ought to observe. Hence, [O believer,] do not let those [who follow ways other than thine] draw thee into disputes on this score, but summon [them all] unto thy Sustainer: for, behold, thou art indeed on the right way. And if they [try to] argue with thee, say [only]: "God knows best what you are doing."

The Qur'an. Al-Hajj (The Pilgrimage) 22:67-68.

ORDER TESTIMONY 2

O you who have attained to faith! Be ever steadfast in upholding equity, bearing witness to the truth for the sake of God, even though it be against your own selves or your parents and kinsfolk. Whether the person concerned be rich or poor, God's claim takes precedence over [the claims of] either of them. Do not, then, follow your own desires, lest you swerve from justice: for if you distort [the truth], or refuse to testify, behold, God is indeed aware of all that you do!

The Qur'an. An-Nisaa (Women) 4:135.

Meher Baba:

Selfless service is accomplished when there is not the slightest thought of reward or result, and when there is complete disregard of one's own comfort or convenience or the possibility of being misunderstood. When you are wholly occupied with the welfare of others, you can hardly think of yourself. You are not concerned with your comfort and convenience or your health and happiness. On the contrary you are willing to sacrifice everything for their well-being. Their comfort is your convenience, their health is your delight, and their happiness is your joy. You find your life in losing it in theirs. You live in their hearts, and your heart becomes their shelter. When there is true union of hearts, you completely identify yourself with the other person. Your act of help or word of comfort supplies to others whatever might be lacking in them; and through their thoughts of gratitude and goodwill, you actually receive more than you give.

Meher Baba, *Discourses*, 7th edition. P. 53–54.

Oh, then, if gleams of truth and light
Flash o'er thy waiting mind,
Unfolding to thy mental sight
The wants of human-kind;
If, brooding over human grief,
The earnest wish is known
To soothe and gladden with relief
An anguish not thine own;

Though heralded with naught of fear,
Or outward sign or show;
Though only to the inward ear
It whispers soft and low;
Though dropping, as the manna fell,
Unseen, yet from above,
Noiseless as dew-fall, heed it well,---
Thy Father's call of love!

John Greenleaf Whittier, "The Call of the Christian," in *The Complete Poetical Works of John Greenleaf Whittier*, p 92.

ORDER PRINCIPLE 3

LOVE IS EMPATHY

To love God in the most practical way is to love our fellow beings. If we feel for others in the same way as we feel for our own dear ones, we love God.

Quakers:

"Now that you may know and feele, the life and the power of Every spirit, knowing the puer Light in your selves, you will com to Saver [savour] the Life in others and that that savors of the Deth, will be deth to the Life…"

Margaret Fell, *Undaunted Zeal: The Letters of Margaret Fell*, "To Brethren and Sisters 1657," p. 239.

"To consider mankind otherwise than brethren, to think favours are peculiar to one nation and exclude others, plainly supposes a darkness in the understanding. For as God's love is universal, so where the mind is sufficiently influenced by it, it begets a likeness of itself and the heart is enlarged towards all men. Again, to conclude a people forward, perverse, and worse by nature than others (who ungratefully receive favours and apply them to bad ends), this will excite a behavior toward them unbecoming the excellence of true religion."

John Woolman, *The Journal and Major Essays of John Woolman*, p 202.

3. LOVE IS EMPATHY

Jesus:

Owe no man any thing, but to love one another: for he that loveth another hath fulfilled the law. For this, Thou shalt not commit adultery, Thou shalt not kill, Thou shalt not steal, Thou shalt not bear false witness, Thou shalt not covet; and if there be any other commandment, it is briefly comprehended in this saying, namely, Thou shalt love thy neighbour as thyself. Love worketh no ill to his neighbour: therefore love is the fulfilling of the law.

Romans 13:8–10 (AV).

Tanakh:

When a stranger resides with you in your land, you shall not wrong him. The stranger who resides with you shall be to you as one of your citizens; you shall love him as yourself, for you were strangers in the land of Egypt: I the Lord am your God.

Tanakh: The Holy Scriptures. Leviticus 19:33-34.

If your enemy is hungry, give him bread to eat;
If he is thirsty, give him water to drink.

Tanakh: The Holy Scriptures. Proverbs 25:21.

Zarathushtra:

Whoso unto the Righteous acteth just,—
      Whether as 'Self-Reliant' he be known,
      Whether 'Co-worker' named, or 'Friend' addressed,—

And whoso fosters zealously all Life,
>He doth assure himself a place within
>The Realm of Knowledge and of Love.

The Divine Songs of Zarathushtra. Ahunavaiti 6.3—Yasna 33.3.

Krishna:

He looks impartially on all:
those who love him or hate him,
his kinsmen, his enemies, his friends,
the good, and also the wicked.

Bhagavad Gita. 6.9.

He who has let go of hatred,
who treats all beings with kindness
and compassion, who is always serene,
unmoved by pain or pleasure,

free of the "I" and "mine,"
self-controlled, firm and patient,
his whole mind focused on me—
that man is the one I love best.

Bhagavad Gita. 12.13–14.

3. LOVE IS EMPATHY

<u>Buddha:</u>

If you examine this precious mind or emotion of altruism, of compassion, you will see that you need an object to generate even this feeling. And that object is a fellow human being. From this point of view, that very precious state of mind, compassion, is impossible without the presence of others....When you think along such lines, you will find sufficient grounds to feel connected with others, to feel the need to repay their kindness.

His Holiness the Dalai Lama; Robert Kiely, ed., *The Good Heart: a Buddhist Perspective on the Teachings of Jesus*. (Somerville, MA: Wisdom Publications, 1998 [paperback]), p. 68.

In light of these convictions, it becomes impossible to believe that some people are totally irrelevant to your life or that you can afford to adopt an indifferent attitude toward them. There are no human beings that are irrelevant to your life.

The Good Heart. P. 68.

<u>Muhammad's Revelation:</u>

And tell My servants that they should speak in the most kindly manner [unto those who do not share their beliefs]: verily, Satan is always ready to stir up discord between men – for, verily, Satan is man's open foe!

The Qur'an. Al-Israa (The Night Journey) 17:53.

ORDER TESTIMONY 3

Meher Baba:

Love is essentially self-communicative; those who do not have it catch it from those who have it. Those who receive love from others cannot be its recipients without giving a response that, in itself, is the nature of love. True love is unconquerable and irresistible. It goes on gathering power and spreading itself until eventually it transforms everyone it touches.

Meher Baba, *Discourses*, 7th edition. P. 9.

The dawn of love facilitates the death of selfishness.

Meher Baba, *Discourses*, 7th edition. P. 13.

If with readier ear thou heedest
    What the Inward Teacher saith,
Listening with a willing spirit
    And a childlike faith, --

Thou mayest live to bless the giver,
    Who, himself but frail and weak,
Would at least the highest welfare
    Of another seek;

And his gift, though poor and lowly
    It may seem to other eyes,
Yet may prove an angel holy
    In a pilgrim's guise.

John Greenleaf Whittier, "To___, With a Copy of Woolman's Journal," in *The Complete Poetical Works of John Greenleaf Whittier*, p 109-111.

ORDER PRINCIPLE 4

LOVE IS GIVING TO OTHERS

If, instead of robbing others to help ourselves, we rob ourselves to help others, we are loving God.

Quakers:

"If there is any one thing more strongly inculcated and enjoined in the testimony of the ancients,... it is the duty of administering to the necessities of the suffering, of giving aid to the weak and perishing. Righteous conduct, right doing, good works, practical righteousness, or whatever name we may apply to it, has been inculcated by the good — the truly pious in all ages of the world."

Lucretia Mott, *Lucretia Mott Speaks: The Essential Speeches and Sermons*, "Cherry Street Meeting, Philadelphia, March 31, 1850," p. 85.

"Our gracious Creator cares and provides for all his creatures. His tender mercies are over all his works; and so far as his love influences our minds, so far as we become interested in his workmanship and feel a desire to take hold of every opportunity to lessen the distresses of the afflicted and increase the happiness of the creation. Here we have a prospect of one common interest from which our own is inseparable – that to turn all the treasures we possess into the channel of universal love becomes the business of our lives."

John Woolman, *The Journal and Major Essays of John Woolman*, "A Plea For The Poor," p 241.

4. LOVE IS GIVING TO OTHERS

Jesus:

Hereby perceive we the love of God, because he laid down his life for us: and we ought to lay down our lives for the brethren. But whoso hath this world's good, and seeth his brother have need, and shutteth up his bowels of compassion from him, how dwelleth the love of God in him?

1 John 3:16–17 (AV).

Tanakh:

One man gives generously and ends with more;
Another stints on doing the right thing and incurs a loss.
A generous person enjoys prosperity;
He who satisfies others shall himself be sated.
He who withholds grain earns the curses of the people,
But blessings are on the head of the one who dispenses it.

Tanakh: The Holy Scriptures. Proverbs 11:24–26.

He who withholds what is due to the poor affronts his Maker;
He who shows pity for the needy honors Him.

Tanakh: The Holy Scriptures. Proverbs 14:31.

Zarathushtra:

As Lords Temporal work their will on Earth,
    So by their gathered Knowledge Teachers wise;
The gifts of Love come as reward
    For deeds done out of Love for Lord of Life;

God's Righteousness surely cometh down
    On him who serves with zeal his brothers meek.

The Divine Songs of Zarathushtra. "Ahuna-Vairya," p. 17 ("Ahuna Vairya" is one of the three daily prayers—"The Three Sacred Verses").

Krishna:

He who acts for my sake,
loving me, free of attachment,
with benevolence toward all beings,
will come to me in the end.

Bhagavad Gita. 11.55.

Charity given to the worthy,
without any expectations,
for the sake of the act itself—
this kind of charity is sattvic.

Bhagavad Gita. 17.20.

Buddha:

May I be a protector for the unprotected;
A guide for travelers on the way;
A boat, a raft, or a bridge
For those who long to cross to the other shore.

4. LOVE IS GIVING TO OTHERS

May I be an isle for those who seek an island;
A lamp for those who wish for light;
A shelter for those in need of rest;
A servant for those in need of service.

Shantideva Bodhicaryavatara 3:17–18, as quoted in: *His Holiness the Dalai Lama, Toward a True Kinship of Faiths* (New York, NY: Three Rivers Press, 2010), p. 61.

Muhammad's Revelation:

True piety does not consist in turning your faces towards the east or the west - but truly pious is he who believes in God ... and spends his substance - however much he himself may cherish it - upon his near of kin, and the orphans, and the needy, and the wayfarer, and the beggars, and for the freeing of human beings from bondage.

The Qur'an. Al-Baqarah (The Cow) 2:177.

Meher Baba:

When a person realizes that he can have more glorious satisfaction by widening the sphere of his interests and activities, he is heading toward the life of service. At this stage he entertains many good desires. He wants to make others happy by relieving distress and helping them.

Meher Baba, *Discourses*, 7th edition. P. 13.

ORDER TESTIMONY 4

..As the person entertains good desires his selfishness embraces a larger conception that eventually brings about its own extinction. Instead of merely trying to be illustrious, arresting, and possessive, he learns to be useful to others.

Meher Baba, *Discourses*, 7th edition. P. 13.

Nor mine the seer-like power to show
The secrets of the heart and mind;
    To drop the plummet-line below
    Our common world of joy and woe,
A more intense despair or brighter hope to find.

    Yet here at least an earnest sense
Of human right and weal is shown;
    A hate of tyranny intense,
    And hearty in its vehemence,
As if my brother's pain and sorrow were my own.

John Greenleaf Whittier, "Prologue Proem," in The Complete Poetical Works of John Greenleaf Whittier, facing page of table of contents.

ORDER PRINCIPLE 5

LOVE IS COMPASSION

If we suffer in the suffering of others and feel happy in the happiness of others, we are loving God.

Quakers:

"Not only is this hope filling the minds of many of the faithful, but they behold the spirit of mercy spreading over the country. — The prisons are visited; insane hospitals are erected for meliorating the condition of suffering humanity; efforts are made to remove the gallows and other barbarous inflictions from our midst; and an increasing regard for the poor and the lowly, leading many to give countenance to systems which shall raise these, and tend to equalize the condition of the human family. If that equality which is our nation's boast were recognized, we should not see large classes, crushed by existing monopolies, laboring for their scanty pittance. True christian democracy and republicanism would lead us not to 'look upon our own things merely, but also upon the things of others.' The practical precept of the Son of God requires, 'whatsoever we would that men should do unto us, even so should we do unto them.'"

Lucretia Mott, Lucretia Mott Speaks: *The Essential Speeches and Sermons*, "'Sermon to the Medical Students, Cherry Street Meeting, Philadelphia, February 11, 1849,'" p. 54.

"...and was early convinced in my mind that true religion consisted in an inward life, wherein the heart doth love and reverence God the Creator and learn to exercise true justice and goodness, not only toward all men but also toward the brute creatures; that as the mind was moved on an inward principle to love God as an invisible, incomprehensible being, on the same

5. LOVE IS COMPASSION

principle it was moved to love him in all his manifestations in the visible world; that as by his breath the flame of life was kindled in all animal and sensitive creatures, to say we love God as unseen and at the same time exercise cruelty toward the least creature moving by his life, or by life derived from him, was a contradiction in itself."

John Woolman, *The Journal and Major Essays of John Woolman*, 1720-1742, p. 28.

"Now that everie particuler member of the body may be sensible of the hardship and sufferings of others and be willinge and serviceable in their places, in what the Lord requires, and to remember those that are in bonds, as bound with them, and them that suffer adversitie, as you beinge your selves also in the bodie, and that you may beare one anothers burdens and be equally yooked in the sufferings...".

Margaret Fell, *Undaunted Zeal: The Letters of Margaret Fell*, "To Friends in The North 1654," p. 90-1.

"I cried to the Lord saying, "Why should I be thus, seeing I was never addicted to commit these evils?" and the Lord answered that it was needful that I have a sense of all conditions, and in this I saw the infinite Love of God. I also saw that there was an ocean of darkness and death, but an infinite ocean of Light and Love which flowed over the ocean of darkness. In that also, I saw the infinite love of God; and I had great openings."

George Fox, *The Journal of George Fox*, "An Ocean of Light and Love," 1649, p. 11.

ORDER TESTIMONY 5

Jesus:

Bear one another's burdens, and so fulfill the law of Christ.

Galatians 6:2 (AV).

If one member suffers, all suffer together; if one member is honored, all rejoice together.

1 Corinthians 12:26 (AV).

Tanakh:

Learn to do good.
Devote yourself to justice;
Aid the wronged.
Uphold the rights of the orphan;
Defend the cause of the widow.

Tanakh: The Holy Scriptures. Isaiah 1:17.

If you banish the yoke from your midst,
The menacing hand, and evil speech,
And you offer your compassion to the hungry
And satisfy the famished creature—
Then shall your light shine in darkness,

And your gloom shall be like noonday.

Tanakh: The Holy Scriptures. Isaiah 58:9-10.

5. LOVE IS COMPASSION

<u>Zarathushtra:</u>

To their Exalted Home shall I, indeed,
    Lead Souls attuned to Love's Love :
Being aware of blessings pouring down
    On deeds performed in God's Name
As long as I have will and wield the pow'r
    I'll teach mankind to love and strive for Truth.

The Divine Songs of Zarathushtra. Ahunavaiti 2.4—Yasna 28.4.

<u>Krishna:</u>

When he sees all beings as equal
in suffering or in joy
because they are like himself,
that man has grown perfect in yoga.

Bhagavad Gita. 6.32.

<u>Buddha:</u>

When a disciple is moved to make objective gifts of charity, he should also practice the Sila Paramita of selfless kindness, that is, he should remember that there is no arbitrary distinction between one's own self and the selfhood of others and, therefore, he should practice charity by giving, not objective gifts alone,

but the selfless gifts of kindness and sympathy.

A Buddhist Bible. P. 91.

Good people walk on, whatever befall; the good do not prattle, longing for pleasure; whether touched by happiness or sorrow, wise people never appear elated or depressed.

The Dhammapada. 6:83.

Muhammad's Revelation:

And what could make thee conceive what it is, that steep uphill road? [It is] the freeing of one's neck [from the burden of sin], or the feeding, upon a day of [one's own] hunger, of an orphan near of kin, or of a needy [stranger] lying in the dust — and being, withal, of those who have attained to faith, and who enjoin upon one another patience in adversity, and enjoin upon one another compassion. Such are they that have attained to righteousness,

The Qur'an. Al-Balad (The Land) 90:12-18.

Meher Baba:

The heart, which in its own way feels the unity of life, wants to fulfill itself through a life of love, sacrifice, and service. It is keen about giving instead of taking. It derives its driving power from the inmost spiritual urge, expressing itself through the immediate intuitions of the inner life ... the heart, feeling in its inner experiences the glow of love, has glimpses of the unity of the spirit and thus seeks expression through self-giving tendencies that unite humanity and make it selfless and generous.

Meher Baba, *Discourses*, 7th edition. P. 95.

Haply from them the toiler, bent
         Above his forge or plough, may gain,
    A manlier spirit of content,
    And feel that life is wisest spent
Where the strong working hand makes strong the working brain.

John Greenleaf Whittier, "Dedication to the Songs of Labor," in *The Complete Poetical Works of John Greenleaf Whittier*, p 112.

ORDER PRINCIPLE 6

DO NOT SHIRK YOUR RESPONSIBILITIES

Quakers:

"While [Jesus] relieved the sufferings of his fellow beings, he at the same time infused his blessed gospel of glad tidings of great joy unto all people, by directing them to that fount within themselves, whence the pure water which springeth up into everlasting life — that heavenly manna which all might partake of — that which cometh down from heaven, from a source higher than earth, and nourishes the immortal soul. He then, never separated his spiritual from his outward duties."

Lucretia Mott, *Lucretia Mott Speaks: The Essential Speeches and Sermons*, "Cherry Street Meeting, Philadelphia, March 31, " 1850," p. 85.

"Silence as to every motion proceeding from the love of money, and an humble waiting upon God to know his will concerning us, hath now appeared necessary. He alone is able to strengthen us to dig deep, to remove all which lies between us and the safe foundation, and so direct us in our outward employments that pure universal love may shine forth in our proceedings."

John Woolman, *The Journal and Major Essays of John Woolman*, p 170-71.

6. DO NOT SHIRK YOUR RESPONSIBILITIES

Jesus:

But this I say, He which soweth sparingly shall reap also sparingly; and he which soweth bountifully shall reap also bountifully. Every man according as he purposeth in his heart, so let him give; not grudgingly, or of necessity: for God loveth a cheerful giver. And God is able to make all grace abound toward you; that ye, always having all sufficiency in all things, may abound to every good work.

2 Corinthians 9:6–8 (AV).

Tanakh:

You represent the people before God: you bring the disputes before God, and enjoin upon them the laws and the teachings, and make known to them the way they are to go and the practices they are to follow.

Tanakh: The Holy Scriptures. Exodus 18:19–20.

Six days you shall labor and do all your work.

Tanakh: The Holy Scriptures. Exodus 20:9.

Zarathushtra:

O Wise Follower of God, I have taught
That action, not inaction, higher stands,
Obeying, then, His Will, worship through deeds;
    The Great Lord, wondrous Guardian of the Worlds,
      Through His Eternal Law discriminates,

ORDER TESTIMONY 6

Who are the truly Wise and who Unwise.

The Divine Songs of Zarathushtra. Ustavaiti 4.17—Yasna 46.17.

Krishna:

Know what your duty is
and do it without hesitation.
For a warrior, there is nothing better
than a battle that duty enjoins.

Bhagavad Gita. 2.31.

Without concern for results,
perform the necessary action;
surrendering all attachments,
accomplish life's highest good.

Bhagavad Gita. 3.19.

Buddha:

He who possesses character and discrimination, who is just, speaks the truth, and does what is his own business, him the world will hold dear.

The Dhammapada. 16:217.

Muhammad's Revelation:

And give full measure whenever you measure, and weigh with a balance that is true: this will be [for your own] good, and best

6. DO NOT SHIRK YOUR RESPONSIBILITIES

in the end.

The Qur'an. Al-'Isrāa' (The Night Journey) 17:35.

Meher Baba:

A real spiritual experience involves not only realization of the nature of the soul while traversing the higher planes of consciousness but also a right attitude toward worldly duties. If it loses its connection with the different phases of life, what we have is a neurotic reaction that is far from being a spiritual experience.

Meher Baba, *Discourses*, 7th edition. P. 6.

ORDER TESTIMONY 6

Our Friend, our Brother, and our Lord,
  What may thy service be? –
Nor name, nor form, nor ritual word,
  But simply following thee.

John Greenleaf Whittier, "Our Master," in *The Complete Poetical Works of John Greenleaf Whittier*, p 319-321.

ORDER PRINCIPLE 7

FIDELITY

If you have the fidelity that your breath has in keeping you company till the end of your life—even without your constantly feeling it, both in happiness and suffering, never turning against you—then you will know Me.

<u>Quakers:</u>

"…And who are faithfull unto the death, a crowne of life & immortality is reserved in the bosome of the father unto such who are truly, & faithfully, & singly given up to his will, And to his worke, & to his service, or to suffer for his names sake."

Margaret Fell, *Undaunted Zeal: The Letters of Margaret Fell*, "To Friends in Prison, with a Postscript by Henry Fell March 5, 1661," p. 340.

"When we look towards the end of life, and think on the division of our substance among our successors, if we know that it was collected in the fear of the Lord, in honesty, inequity, and in uprightness of heart before him, we may consider it as his gift to us, and with a single eye to his blessing, bestow it on those we leave behind us. Such is the happiness of the plain ways of true virtue. "The work of righteousness shall be peace; and the effect of righteousness, quitness, and assurance forever. (Isaiah 32:17)"

John Woolman, *The Journal of John Woolman (HC)*, 1758, p. 211.

7. FIDELITY

Jesus:

"For verily I say unto you, Till heaven and earth pass, one jot or one tittle shall in no wise pass from the law, till all be fulfilled."

Matthew 5:18 (AV).

Tanakh:

Therefore impress these My words upon your very heart: bind them as a sign on your hand and let them serve as a symbol on your forehead, and teach them to your children—reciting them when you stay at home and when you are away, when you lie down and when you get up; and inscribe them on the doorposts of your house and on your gates—to the end that you and your children may endure, in the land that the Lord swore to your fathers to assign to them, as long as there is a heaven over the earth.

Tanakh: The Holy Scriptures. Deuteronomy 11:18-21.

Let fidelity and steadfastness not leave you;
Bind them about your throat,
Write them on the tablet of your mind,
And you will find favor and approbation
In the eyes of God and man.

Tanakh: The Holy Scriptures. Proverbs 3:3-4.

Zarathushtra:

His favour will I seek and Love's,
For in His Plan are found both weal and woe.

The Divine Songs of Zarathushtra. Ustavaiti 3.9—Yasna 45.9.

Krishna:

Only by single-minded
devotion can I be known
as I truly am, Arjuna—
can I be seen and entered.

Bhagavad Gita. 11.54.

Those who love and revere me
with unwavering faith, always
centering their minds on me—
they are the most perfect in yoga.

Bhagavad Gita. 12.2.

Buddha:

The disciples of Gotama are always wide awake and watchful,
and their thoughts day and night are ever set on Buddha.

The disciples of Gotama are always wide awake and watchful,
and their thoughts day and night are ever set on the Law.

The disciples of Gotama are always wide awake and watchful,
and their thoughts day and night are ever set on

7. FIDELITY

the Order.

The disciples of Gotama are always wide awake and watchful, and their thoughts day and night are ever set on the body.

The disciples of Gotama are always wide awake and watchful, and their mind day and night ever delights in compassion.

The Dhammapada. 21:296–300.

Muhammad's Revelation:

Verily, those who have attained to faith and do good works, and are constant in prayer, and dispense charity – they shall have their reward with their Sustainer, and no fear need they have, and neither shall they grieve.

The Qur'an. Al-Baqarah (The Cow) 2:277.

And when Jesus became aware of their refusal to acknowledge the truth, he asked: "Who will be my helpers in God's cause?" The white-garbed ones replied: "We shall be [thy] helpers [in the cause] of God! We believe in God: and bear thou witness that we have surrendered ourselves unto Him! O our Sustainer! We believe in what Thou hast bestowed from on high, and we follow this Apostle; make us one, then, with all who bear witness [to the truth]!"

The Qur'an. 'Āl-'Imrān (The House of 'Imrān) 3:52–53.

Meher Baba:

To avoid defeat, the mind must stick tenaciously to the right values it has perceived. Thus the solution of mental conflict requires not only perception of right values but also an unswerving fidelity to them.

Meher Baba, *Discourses*, 7th edition. P. 163-164.

Acknowledgments

Laurent Weichberger, who will ever be first in acknowledgement, for it was he who put the fire in the project in the beginning:

> "A service Thy service cannot tire,
> A Faith which doubt can never dim,
> A heart of Love, a lip of fire,
> O Freedom's God! Be thou to him."

From *A Letter to a Young Clerical Friend*
"Voices of Freedom,"
Whittier 1846

Megan Lanier, who tirelessly prepared and edited the content, as well as persevering with learning InDesign software for the formatting:

> "So wisely taught the Indian seer;
> Destroying Shiva, Forming Brahma,
> Who woke by turns Earth's Love and fear,
> Are One, the same".

"The Reformer,"
Whittier 1849

Annapolis Library Committee, a/k/a "The Happy Committee":

> "Nor lack I Friends, long tried, and near and dear,
> Whose Love around me like this atmosphere,
> Warm, soft, and golden. For such gifts to me

ACKNOWLEDGEMENTS

What shall I render O God to thee"?

"The Prisoner of Naples,"
Whitter 1852

Freedom Francis Wayne, whose use of this book for Quaker Bible Study at Annapolis Friends Monthly set the standard for depth in finding common InterFaith Testimonies."

> "The Quaker of the Olden time!
> How calm and firm and true,
> Unspotted by its wrong and crime,
> He walked the dark earth through.
> Around him had no power to stain
> the purity within."

"The Quaker of the Olden Time,"
Whittier 1849

Sheila Gambill, "Eagle Eyed Editor," who consistently kept to the task at hand of editing as WhittIer says, without "any sign of haste or carelessness":

> "And hence my pen unfettered moves,
> In freedom which the heart approves,
> The negligence which Friendship loves,
> And wilt thou prize my poor gift less
> For simple air and rustic dress
> And sign of haste and carelessness"?

"Lines Written in a Book of a Friend,"
Whittier 1845

ACKNOWLEDGEMENTS

Sufi Karl Moeller for the illuminated cover:

> "That which mystic Plato pondered
> That which Zeno heard with awe
> And the star rapt Zoroaster
> In His night watch saw."

"To_____ With a Copy of Woolman's Journal"
Whittier 1849

To Coinegean Greenwalker:

So sweet, So dear is the silvery tone,
Of her in whose features I sometimes look,
As I sit By Her side alone,
And we read by turns from the self-same book,
Some tale perhaps of the olden time,
Some lover's romance or quaint old rhyme.
Whittier The Demon of the Study

APPENDIX A

Meher Baba's Original 33 Principles

THE SEVEN REALITIES

Meher Baba's teaching gives no importance to creed, dogma, caste or the performance of religious ceremonies and rites, but does to the UNDERSTANDING of the following seven Realities:

1. The only Real Existence is that of the One and only God Who is the Self in every (finite) self. [**Truth** 1]
2. The only Real Love is the Love for this Infinity (God), which arouses an intense longing to see, know and become one with its Truth (God). [**Order** 1]
3. The only Real Sacrifice is that in which, in pursuance of this Love, all things—body, mind, position, welfare and even life itself—are sacrificed. [**Equality** 1]
4. The only Real Renunciation is that which abandons, even in the midst of worldly duties, all selfish thoughts and desires. [**Simplicity** 1]
5. The only Real Knowledge is the Knowledge that God is the inner dweller in good people and in so-called bad, in saint and in so-called sinner. This Knowledge requires you to help all equally as circumstances demand without expectation of reward, and when compelled to take part in a dispute, to act without the slightest trace of enmity or hatred; to try to make others happy with brotherly or sisterly feeling for each one; and to harm no one in thought, word or deed, not even those who harm you. [**Order** 2]
6. The only Real Control is the discipline of the senses to abstain from indulgence in low desires, which alone ensures absolute purity of character. [**Simplicity** 2]
7. The only Real Surrender is that in which poise is undisturbed by any adverse circumstance, and the individual, amidst every kind of hardship, is resigned with perfect calm to the will of God. [**Peace** 2]

HOW TO LOVE GOD

8. To love God in the most practical way is to love our fellow beings. If we feel for others in the same way as we feel for our own dear ones, we love God. [**Order** 3]

9. If, instead of seeing faults in others, we look within ourselves, we are loving God. [**Equality** 2]

10. If, instead of robbing others to help ourselves, we rob ourselves to help others, we are loving God. [**Order** 4]

11. If we suffer in the sufferings of others and feel happy in the happiness of others, we are loving God. [**Order** 5]

12. If, instead of worrying over our own misfortunes, we think ourselves more fortunate than many many others, we are loving God. [**Equality** 3]

13. If we endure our lot with patience and contentment, accepting it as His Will, we are loving God. [**Peace** 3]

14. If we understand and feel that the greatest act of devotion and worship to God is not to hurt or harm any of His beings, we are loving God. [**Peace** 4]

15. To love God as He ought to be loved, we must live for God and die for God, knowing that the goal of life is to Love God, and find Him as our own self. [**Truth** 2]

THE PATH OF LOVE, p. 109
Copyright 1986 Avatar Meher Baba Perpetual Public Charitable Trust

MY WISH

The lover has to keep the wish of the Beloved. My wish for my lovers is as follows:

16. Do not shirk your responsibilities. [**Order** 6]
17. Attend faithfully to your worldly duties, but keep always at the back of your mind that all this is Baba's. [**Simplicity** 3]
18. When you feel happy, think: "Baba wants me to be happy." When you suffer, think: "Baba wants me to suffer." [**Peace** 5]
19. Be resigned to every situation and think honestly and sincerely: "Baba has placed me in this situation." [**Simplicity** 4]
20. With the understanding that Baba is in everyone, try to help and serve others. [**Equality** 4]
21. I say with my Divine Authority to each and all that whosoever takes my name at the time of breathing his last comes to me; so do not forget to remember me in your last moments. Unless you start remembering me from now on, it will be difficult to remember me when your end approaches. You should start practising from now on. Even if you take my name only once every day, you will not forget to remember me in your dying moments. [**Truth** 3]

GOD-MAN, p. 320, C. B. Purdom
1971 © Meher Spiritual Center, Inc.

TWELVE WAYS OF REALIZING ME

22. Longing
If you experience that same longing and thirst for union with Me as one who has been lying for days in the hot sun of the Sahara experiences the longing for water, then you will realize Me. [**Truth** 4]

23. Peace of Mind
If you have the peace of a frozen lake, then too you will realize Me. [**Peace** 1]

24. Humility
If you have the humility of the earth, which can be molded into any shape, then you will know Me. [**Equality** 5]

25. Desperation
If you experience the desperation that causes a person to commit suicide and you feel that you cannot live without seeing Me, then you will see Me. [**Truth** 5]

26. Faith
If you have the complete faith that Kalyan had in his Master—in believing it was night although it was day because his Master said so—then you will know Me. [**Truth** 6]

27. Fidelity
If you have the fidelity that your breath has in keeping you company until the end of your life—even without your constantly feeling it, both in happiness and suffering, never turning against you—then you will know Me. [**Order** 7]

28. Control through Love
When your love for Me drives away your lust for things of the senses, then you will realize Me. [**Simplicity** 5]

29. Selfless Service
If you have the quality of selfless service unaffected by results similar to that of the sun, which serves the world by shining on all creation—on the grass in the field, on the birds in the air, on the beasts in the forest, on all of mankind with its sinners and

saints, its rich and poor—unmindful of the attitude toward it, then you will win Me. [**Equality** 6]

30. Renunciation

If you renounce for Me everything physical, mental, and spiritual, then you will have Me. [**Simplicity** 6]

31. Obedience

If your obedience is as spontaneous, complete, and natural as light is to the eye or smell is to the nose, then you will come to Me. [**Simplicity** 7]

32. Surrender

If your surrender to Me is as wholehearted as that of one who, suffering from insomnia, surrenders to sudden sleep without fear of being lost, then you will have Me. [**Truth** 7]

33. Love

If you have that love for Me that Saint Francis has for Jesus, then not only will you realize Me but you will please Me. [**Peace** 6]

Meher Baba's Discourses, Epilogue

www.ingramcontent.com/pod-product-compliance
Lightning Source LLC
Chambersburg PA
CBHW030547080526
44585CB00012B/286